I0409336

# Contents

# 1. Chapter 1

## Setting the Foundation

In this chapter, we delve into the importance of cultivating a wealthy mindset as the first step towards financial success. We explore how our thoughts and beliefs shape our financial reality and discuss strategies for adopting a positive and abundance-oriented mindset. We then guide readers through the process of defining their financial goals and vision, helping them articulate what they want to achieve financially. Next, we encourage readers to assess their current financial situation, examining their income, expenses, assets, and liabilities. Finally, we emphasize the significance of building a solid financial plan that aligns with their goals and serves as a roadmap for their journey.

### 1.1    The Power of a Wealthy Mindset

In the journey towards financial success, one of the most crucial factors that often goes overlooked is the power of mindset. Your mindset shapes your beliefs, attitudes, and behaviors, and ultimately determines your financial trajectory. A wealthy mindset is not limited to the rich and successful; it is a mindset that anyone can adopt, regardless of their current financial situation. In this chapter, we will explore the power of a wealthy mindset, understand its key components, and discover how it can transform your relationship with money and pave the way for financial abundance.

**The Foundation of a Wealthy Mindset:**

At the core of a wealthy mindset is a deep-rooted belief in abundance. It is the understanding that the universe is abundant, and there are unlimited opportunities for financial success. This belief lays the foundation for a positive and optimistic outlook towards money and wealth creation. We will explore techniques to cultivate this belief, including gratitude practices, visualization exercises, and positive affirmations.

**Shifting from Scarcity to Abundance:**

Many individuals operate from a scarcity mindset, where they constantly worry about lack, competition, and scarcity of resources. However, a wealthy mindset requires a shift from scarcity to abundance thinking. We will delve into the key differences between these mindsets and provide practical strategies to reframe scarcity-based thoughts and embrace abundance as a default mode of thinking.

**Overcoming Limiting Beliefs:**

Limiting beliefs act as mental barriers that hinder our progress towards financial success. They are often deeply ingrained in our subconscious and hold us back from taking risks, pursuing opportunities, and stepping outside our comfort zones. We will identify common limiting beliefs around money and wealth and offer techniques to challenge and replace them with empowering beliefs that support our financial growth.

**Embracing a Growth Mindset:**

A growth mindset is essential for fostering continuous learning, adaptability, and resilience on the path to financial success. We will explore the concept of a growth mindset and its impact on our ability to embrace challenges, learn from failures, and persist in the face of setbacks. Practical strategies, such as reframing failure as feedback and cultivating a love for learning, will be discussed to help nurture a growth mindset.

**Developing Financial Confidence and Self-Worth:**

A wealthy mindset is also closely tied to our sense of self-worth and confidence in managing finances. We will discuss techniques to build financial confidence, including financial education, goal setting, and tracking progress. Additionally, we will explore the connection between self-worth and wealth, emphasizing the importance of valuing oneself independent of financial status and understanding that wealth is a byproduct of inner worth.

**Cultivating an Abundance Mentality:**

An abundance mentality goes beyond material wealth and encompasses a holistic approach to life. We will discuss the principles of an abundance mentality, such as generosity, collaboration, and gratitude. By cultivating these qualities, we can attract more opportunities, build meaningful relationships, and create a positive ripple effect in our financial journey and beyond.

**Mindfulness and Financial Decision-Making:**

Mindfulness plays a vital role in developing a wealthy mindset. By practicing mindfulness, we can cultivate awareness of our thoughts, emotions, and impulses related to money. This awareness empowers us to make conscious financial decisions aligned with our long-term goals and values. We will explore mindfulness techniques, such as meditation and mindful spending, to enhance our financial decision-making process.

**Surrounding Yourself with Abundance:**

The people we surround ourselves with have a significant influence on our mindset and beliefs. We will discuss the importance of cultivating a supportive network of individuals who embody a wealthy mindset. Additionally, we will explore the impact of our physical environment on our mindset and provide tips for creating an environment that fosters abundance and financial growth.

**Conclusion:**

A wealthy mindset is a powerful tool that can transform your relationship with money, propel you towards financial success, and bring fulfillment and purpose to your life. By embracing abundance, shifting limiting beliefs, and cultivating positive attitudes and behaviors, you can unleash the full potential of your financial journey. Remember, wealth is not just about the money in your bank account; it is about the mindset you bring to every aspect of your life. Embrace the power of a wealthy mindset and unlock a world of possibilities and prosperity.

## 1.2 Defining Your Financial Goals and Vision

Setting clear financial goals and establishing a compelling vision for your financial future is crucial in shaping the direction of your journey towards success. Without a roadmap or destination in mind, it's easy to become lost or stagnant in your financial endeavors. In this chapter, we will delve into the process of defining your financial goals and vision, exploring the significance of clarity, alignment, and purpose. By the end, you will have a solid understanding of how to articulate your financial aspirations and create a roadmap that propels you towards their achievement.

**The Importance of Setting Financial Goals:**

Financial goals act as guideposts, providing direction and motivation in your pursuit of financial success. We will discuss the importance of setting specific, measurable, achievable, relevant, and time-bound (SMART) goals. By outlining your desired financial outcomes, you can create a clear focus and leverage the power of intention to manifest your dreams into reality.

**Reflecting on Personal Values and Priorities:**

Defining your financial goals should be deeply rooted in your personal values and priorities. We will explore techniques for self-reflection, such as identifying your core values and understanding what truly matters to you. By aligning your financial goals with your values, you can create a sense of purpose and meaning in your journey towards financial success.

**Short-Term vs. Long-Term Goals:**

Financial goals can be categorized into short-term and long-term objectives. We will discuss the importance of balancing immediate needs and desires with long-term financial security. By distinguishing between short-term gratification and long-term sustainability, you can prioritize your goals effectively and create a comprehensive plan that accounts for both horizons.

**Creating S.M.A.R.T. Financial Goals:**

To ensure the effectiveness and achievability of your financial goals, we will dive deeper into the SMART framework. We will explore each component, discussing how to make your goals specific, measurable, achievable, relevant, and time-bound. Through practical examples and exercises, you will learn how to craft SMART financial goals that serve as actionable steps towards your vision.

**Goal-Setting Strategies and Techniques:**

Setting goals is not merely an exercise in wishful thinking; it requires a strategic approach. We will explore various goal-setting techniques, such as chunking, visualization, and creating accountability structures. Additionally, we will discuss the power of writing down your goals, tracking progress, and making adjustments along the way to stay on course.

**Financial Vision: Painting a Picture of Your Ideal Future:**

While goals provide specific targets, a financial vision encapsulates your ideal future state. We will guide you through the process of creating a vivid and compelling vision that excites and inspires you. By painting a detailed picture of the lifestyle, experiences, and achievements you desire, you can infuse your financial journey with passion and purpose.

**Aligning Goals with Lifestyle Design:**

Financial goals should not exist in isolation but should be integrated into your overall lifestyle design. We will explore how your goals can align with your desired lifestyle, including factors such as work-life balance, travel, hobbies, and philanthropy. By harmonizing your financial objectives with your ideal lifestyle, you can create a sense of harmony and fulfillment.

**Breaking Down Goals into Actionable Steps:**

To bridge the gap between vision and reality, we will discuss the importance of breaking down your goals into actionable steps. We will explore techniques such as backward planning, creating milestones, and setting priorities. By deconstructing your goals, you can establish a roadmap that outlines the specific actions required to achieve each objective.

**Reviewing and Revising Your Financial Goals:**

Financial goals are not set in stone but evolve as circumstances change. We will emphasize the significance of regularly reviewing and revising your goals to ensure their continued relevance and alignment with your evolving aspirations. We will discuss strategies for tracking progress, celebrating milestones, and making adjustments when necessary.

**Conclusion:**

Defining your financial goals and vision is a fundamental step in shaping your financial future. By setting clear and compelling objectives, rooted in your values and aligned with your desired lifestyle, you create a roadmap that guides you towards success. Remember, goals without action are merely dreams; it's the actions you take that transform your financial reality. Embrace the process of defining your financial goals and vision, and let it propel you towards a future of abundance, fulfillment, and financial freedom.

## 1.3        Assessing Your Current Financial Situation

Before embarking on any financial journey, it is essential to have a comprehensive understanding of your current financial situation. Assessing your financial position provides you with a realistic starting point and enables you to make informed decisions and set appropriate goals. In this chapter, we will explore the process of assessing your current financial situation, covering key areas such as income, expenses, assets, liabilities, and net worth. By the end, you will have a clear picture of your financial standing, empowering you to take proactive steps towards achieving your financial aspirations.

**Gathering Financial Information:**

The first step in assessing your financial situation is to gather all relevant financial information. This includes collecting documentation related to your income, such as pay stubs, freelance income, or investment returns. You should also compile records of your expenses, including bills, loan payments, and other financial obligations. Additionally, gather information on your assets, such as savings accounts, investments, real estate, and retirement accounts, as well as your liabilities, including mortgages, loans, and credit card debt.

### Calculating Your Income:

Understanding your income is crucial in assessing your financial situation. Calculate your total monthly income by considering all sources of revenue, including salaries, bonuses, side gigs, rental income, or investment income. By examining your income, you gain insights into your earning capacity and potential areas for improvement or diversification.

### Analyzing Your Expenses:

Analyzing your expenses is a critical component of assessing your financial situation. Categorize your expenses into fixed (e.g., rent/mortgage, utilities, loan payments) and variable (e.g., groceries, dining out, entertainment). Track your spending habits for a designated period, such as a month, to identify areas where you may be overspending or where you can make adjustments to align with your financial goals.

### Evaluating Your Savings and Emergency Fund:

Assessing your savings and emergency fund is essential for financial security. Calculate the amount you have saved and evaluate whether it aligns with your short-term and long-term financial goals. Determine if your emergency fund is adequate to cover unexpected expenses or income disruptions. If necessary, develop a plan to increase your savings and emergency fund contributions.

**Assessing Your Assets:**

Reviewing your assets provides insights into your overall financial health and net worth. Assess the value of your assets, including cash, investments, real estate, and other valuable possessions. Consider factors such as appreciation, liquidity, and diversification to determine the effectiveness of your asset allocation strategy.

**Understanding Your Liabilities:**

Liabilities, such as debts and loans, have a significant impact on your financial situation. Evaluate your outstanding debts, including mortgages, student loans, credit card debt, and personal loans. Analyze the interest rates, repayment terms, and monthly payments associated with each liability. Understanding your liabilities helps you prioritize debt repayment strategies and manage your overall financial obligations.

**Calculating Your Net Worth:**

Net worth is a key indicator of your financial health and progress towards your goals. Calculate your net worth by subtracting your total liabilities from your total assets. This figure represents the true value of your financial position and provides a baseline for measuring future growth and improvement.

**Assessing Your Risk Tolerance:**

Understanding your risk tolerance is essential for making informed investment decisions and managing financial uncertainties. Assess your comfort level with risk by considering factors such as your financial goals, time horizon, and emotional response to market fluctuations. This assessment will guide you in determining an investment strategy that aligns with your risk tolerance and financial objectives.

**Identifying Financial Strengths and Weaknesses:**

Through the process of assessing your financial situation, you will identify your financial strengths and weaknesses. Assess your ability to generate income, manage expenses, save, invest, and reduce debt. Identifying strengths allows you to leverage them to achieve your financial goals, while identifying weaknesses enables you to address them strategically.

**Seeking Professional Guidance:**

If you find the process of assessing your financial situation overwhelming or if you require expertise in certain areas, consider seeking professional guidance from a financial advisor or planner. They can provide personalized insights, offer strategies to improve your financial situation, and assist in developing a comprehensive financial plan.

**Conclusion:**

Assessing your current financial situation is the foundation of your financial journey. By gathering and analyzing information about your income, expenses, assets, liabilities, and net worth, you gain a holistic understanding of your financial health. This assessment empowers you to identify areas for improvement, set realistic goals, and make informed financial decisions. Remember, assessing your financial situation is not a one-time exercise but an ongoing process as your circumstances change. Regularly revisit and update your assessment to ensure you stay on track towards achieving your financial aspirations.

## 1.4    Building a Solid Financial Plan

A solid financial plan serves as a roadmap for achieving your financial goals and securing your financial future. It encompasses various aspects, including budgeting, saving, investing, risk management, and retirement planning. In this chapter, we will explore the process of building a solid financial plan, step by step. By the end, you will have a comprehensive understanding of how to create a personalized financial plan that aligns with your goals, values, and aspirations.

**Set Clear Financial Goals:**

The foundation of any financial plan is setting clear and specific goals. Define your short-term, medium-term, and long-term financial objectives. Ensure that your goals are realistic, measurable, and time-bound. Examples of financial goals include saving for a down payment on a house, paying off debt, funding education, building an emergency fund, and planning for retirement.

**Assess Your Current Financial Situation:**

Before moving forward, assess your current financial situation. Review your income, expenses, assets, liabilities, and net worth. Understand your cash flow, evaluate your savings and investment accounts, and analyze your debt obligations. This assessment will provide insights into areas that require attention and guide your decision-making process.

**Develop a Budget:**

A budget is a crucial tool in managing your finances effectively. Create a detailed budget that outlines your income and expenses. Allocate your income towards necessities, savings, debt repayment, and discretionary spending. Regularly track and review your budget to ensure you stay on track and make adjustments as needed.

**Establish an Emergency Fund:**

An emergency fund is a safety net for unexpected financial emergencies. Aim to save three to six months' worth of living expenses in a separate, easily accessible account. This fund provides financial security and prevents the need to rely on credit cards or loans during challenging times.

**Manage and Reduce Debt:**

Develop a strategy to manage and reduce your debt. Prioritize high-interest debt, such as credit card debt, and create a plan to pay it off systematically. Consider debt consolidation or refinancing options to lower interest rates and simplify repayment. Minimize new debt and focus on living within your means.

**Save for Short-Term and Medium-Term Goals:**

Allocate a portion of your income towards saving for short-term and medium-term goals. These may include saving for a vacation, a car, or a home down payment. Determine the amount you need to save and establish a timeline. Automate savings by setting up automatic transfers to a dedicated savings account.

**Plan for Retirement:**

Plan for your retirement early to ensure financial security in your later years. Determine your desired retirement age, estimate your future expenses, and calculate the amount you need to save for retirement. Explore retirement savings options, such as employer-sponsored retirement plans (e.g., 401(k)) and individual retirement accounts (IRAs). Contribute regularly and take advantage of any employer matching contributions.

**Implement a Diversified Investment Strategy:**

Investing plays a vital role in building wealth over the long term. Develop a diversified investment strategy that aligns with your risk tolerance and financial goals. Consider a mix of asset classes, such as stocks, bonds, real estate, and mutual funds. Regularly review and rebalance your investment portfolio based on your risk profile and market conditions.

**Protect Yourself with Insurance:**

Insurance is a crucial aspect of financial planning. Assess your insurance needs, including health insurance, life insurance, disability insurance, and property insurance. Determine the coverage required to protect yourself, your loved ones, and your assets. Regularly review your policies and make adjustments as necessary.

**Consider Tax Planning Strategies:**

Tax planning is essential in maximizing your after-tax income and optimizing your financial plan. Stay informed about relevant tax laws and regulations. Utilize tax-efficient investment vehicles, such as retirement accounts and tax-advantaged savings accounts. Consider consulting with a tax professional to identify potential deductions, credits, and strategies that minimize your tax liability.

**Regularly Review and Adjust Your Financial Plan:**

A solid financial plan is not a set-it-and-forget-it document. Regularly review and adjust your plan as your financial situation evolves or as external factors change. Set aside dedicated time each year to assess your progress, update your goals, and make necessary adjustments to your strategies.

**Seek Professional Guidance:**

Building a financial plan can be complex, and it may be beneficial to seek professional guidance from a financial advisor or planner. A qualified professional can provide personalized advice, help you navigate investment options, and ensure your plan aligns with your goals and risk tolerance.

**Conclusion:**

Building a solid financial plan requires careful consideration of your goals, current situation, and various components of personal finance. By setting clear goals, budgeting effectively, managing debt, saving, investing, and protecting yourself through insurance, you can create a robust financial plan that aligns with your aspirations. Remember, a financial plan is dynamic and should be regularly reviewed and adjusted as needed. With a solid financial plan in place, you can navigate financial challenges, work towards your goals, and secure your financial future.

# 2. Chapter 2

## Mastering Personal Finance

Here, we provide practical advice on budgeting and managing expenses effectively. We discuss the importance of tracking income and expenditures, creating a budget, and making conscious spending choices. We also explore various saving strategies, such as automating savings, setting up emergency funds, and utilizing different savings vehicles. Additionally, we offer insights into managing debt, including tips for reducing debt, negotiating interest rates, and prioritizing repayments. We highlight the significance of maintaining a good credit score and provide guidance on how to achieve it.

### 2.1    Budgeting and Managing Expenses

Saving is a fundamental aspect of financial growth and security. It allows you to accumulate wealth, achieve financial goals, and have a safety net for unexpected expenses. In this chapter, we will explore various saving strategies that can help you maximize your savings, optimize your financial growth, and set a strong foundation for your financial future. By implementing these strategies, you can develop healthy saving habits and make your money work for you.

**Set Clear Savings Goals:**

Setting clear savings goals is essential for staying motivated and focused. Define your short-term, medium-term, and long-term savings goals. Examples may include building an emergency fund, saving for a down payment on a house, funding education, or planning for retirement. Ensure that your goals are specific, measurable, achievable, relevant, and time-bound (SMART).

**Create a Budget:**

A budget is a crucial tool in managing your finances effectively and maximizing your savings. Analyze your income and expenses and create a budget that aligns with your financial goals. Allocate a portion of your income towards savings. Track your expenses and identify areas where you can cut back or make adjustments to increase your savings rate.

**Automate Your Savings:**

Automating your savings is a powerful strategy that ensures consistent contributions without relying on willpower alone. Set up automatic transfers from your checking account to a dedicated savings account. This way, a portion of your income is saved before you have a chance to spend it. Consider setting up separate savings accounts for different goals to track progress effectively.

**Pay Yourself First:**

The "pay yourself first" principle involves prioritizing your savings before allocating funds to other expenses. Treat your savings contributions as non-negotiable expenses. Aim to save a percentage of your income with each paycheck, even if it's a small amount initially. Over time, increase your savings rate as you adjust your budget and reduce unnecessary expenses.

**Track and Reduce Your Expenses:**

Regularly track and review your expenses to identify areas where you can reduce unnecessary spending. Analyze your spending patterns and identify discretionary expenses that can be trimmed. Look for opportunities to cut back on subscriptions, dining out, entertainment, and impulse purchases. Redirect the money saved towards your savings goals.

**Practice Frugality:**

Adopting a frugal lifestyle can significantly impact your savings. Embrace frugal habits such as buying in bulk, comparison shopping, using coupons or discounts, and opting for generic brands. Reduce energy consumption, lower utility bills, and limit unnecessary expenses. Cultivate mindful spending habits and question every purchase to determine its true value and necessity.

**Minimize Debt:**

Debt can hinder your ability to save and grow financially. Prioritize debt repayment to free up cash flow for savings. Develop a debt repayment strategy, such as the snowball or avalanche method, to pay off debts systematically. Avoid incurring new debt and practice responsible credit card usage. Redirect the money saved from debt payments towards savings.

**Trim Your Housing Costs:**

Housing expenses often represent a significant portion of your budget. Explore ways to reduce housing costs, such as downsizing, refinancing your mortgage to secure a lower interest rate, or considering roommates to share expenses. Alternatively, explore the possibility of homeownership if renting is costing you more in the long run.

**Maximize Retirement Contributions:**

Contributing to retirement accounts is a powerful way to save for the future while benefiting from tax advantages. Maximize your contributions to employer-sponsored retirement plans, such as a 401(k) or 403(b), especially if your employer offers a matching contribution. Additionally, consider opening an individual retirement account (IRA) to supplement your retirement savings.

**Cut Back on Transportation Expenses:**

Transportation costs can eat into your budget. Consider alternatives to reduce transportation expenses, such as carpooling, using public transportation, biking, or walking for short distances. Explore the possibility of downsizing to one vehicle or even living car-free if feasible. Redirect the money saved towards savings.

**Increase Your Income:**

Increasing your income can accelerate your savings growth. Explore opportunities for a salary increase, negotiate for higher pay, or seek additional income streams through part-time work, freelance gigs, or a side business. Direct the extra income towards savings to supercharge your financial growth.

**Take Advantage of Savings Accounts and Investments:**

Explore different savings accounts and investment options that can grow your money over time. Research high-yield savings accounts, certificates of deposit (CDs), or money market accounts that offer competitive interest rates. Consider investing in low-cost index funds, stocks, bonds, or real estate investment trusts

(REITs) to potentially earn higher returns over the long term.

**Review and Adjust Your Savings Strategy:**

Regularly review and adjust your savings strategy as your financial situation evolves. Revisit your goals, assess your progress, and make necessary adjustments to your savings rate or allocation. Stay informed about new savings opportunities or investment options that may align better with your objectives.

**Conclusion:**

Implementing effective saving strategies is vital for financial growth and stability. By setting clear goals, creating a budget, automating savings, reducing expenses, practicing frugality, minimizing debt, and maximizing retirement contributions, you can optimize your savings and accelerate your journey towards financial success. Remember, building a strong savings habit takes time and discipline. Stay committed to your goals, track your progress, and make adjustments along the way. With consistent effort, you can build a solid financial foundation and achieve your financial aspirations.

## 2.2 Saving Strategies for Financial Growth

Saving is a fundamental aspect of financial growth and security. It allows individuals to accumulate wealth, achieve financial goals, and have a safety net for unexpected expenses. In this chapter, we will explore various saving strategies that can help individuals maximize their savings, optimize their financial growth, and set a strong foundation for their financial future. By implementing these strategies, individuals can develop healthy saving habits and make their money work for them.

**Set Clear Savings Goals:**

Setting clear savings goals is essential for staying motivated and focused. Individuals should define their short-term, medium-term, and long-term savings goals. Examples may include building an emergency fund, saving for a down payment on a house, funding education, or planning for retirement. Ensure that the goals are specific, measurable, achievable, relevant, and time-bound (SMART).

### Create a Budget:

A budget is a crucial tool in managing finances effectively and maximizing savings. Individuals should analyze their income and expenses and create a budget that aligns with their financial goals. They should allocate a portion of their income towards savings. Tracking expenses and identifying areas where they can cut back or make adjustments will increase their savings rate.

### Automate Your Savings:

Automating savings is a powerful strategy that ensures consistent contributions without relying on willpower alone. Setting up automatic transfers from a checking account to a dedicated savings account ensures that a portion of the income is saved before individuals have a chance to spend it. Consider setting up separate savings accounts for different goals to track progress effectively.

### Pay Yourself First:

The "pay yourself first" principle involves prioritizing savings before allocating funds to other expenses. Treating savings contributions as non-negotiable expenses is crucial. Aim to save a percentage of the income with each paycheck, even if it's a small amount initially. Over time, increase the savings rate as individuals adjust their budgets and reduce unnecessary expenses.

**Track and Reduce Expenses:**

Regularly tracking and reviewing expenses helps individuals identify areas where they can reduce unnecessary spending. Analyzing spending patterns and identifying discretionary expenses that can be trimmed are essential steps. They should look for opportunities to cut back on subscriptions, dining out, entertainment, and impulse purchases. The money saved should be redirected towards savings.

**Practice Frugality:**

Adopting a frugal lifestyle can significantly impact savings. Embracing frugal habits such as buying in bulk, comparison shopping, using coupons or discounts, and opting for generic brands is important. Reducing energy consumption, lowering utility bills, and limiting unnecessary expenses are other ways to practice frugality. Cultivating mindful spending habits and questioning every purchase to determine its true value and necessity are key.

**Minimize Debt:**

Debt can hinder the ability to save and grow financially. Prioritizing debt repayment frees up cash flow for savings. Developing a debt repayment strategy, such as the snowball or avalanche method, to pay off debts systematically is important. Avoid incurring new debt and practice responsible credit card usage. The money saved from debt payments should be redirected towards savings.

**Trim Housing Costs:**

Housing expenses often represent a significant portion of a budget. Exploring ways to reduce housing costs, such as downsizing, refinancing a mortgage to secure a lower interest rate, or considering roommates to share expenses, is important. Alternatively, considering homeownership if renting is costing more in the long run is another option.

**Maximize Retirement Contributions:**

Contributing to retirement accounts is a powerful way to save for the future while benefiting from tax advantages. Individuals should maximize their contributions to employer-sponsored retirement plans, such as a 401(k) or 403(b), especially if their employer offers a matching contribution. Additionally, they should consider opening an individual retirement account (IRA) to supplement their retirement savings.

**Explore High-Yield Savings Accounts and Investments:**

Traditional savings accounts often offer low-interest rates, limiting the growth potential of savings. Exploring high-yield savings accounts that offer competitive interest rates is beneficial. Furthermore, individuals should consider investing their savings in low-cost index funds, stocks, bonds, or real estate investment trusts (REITs) to potentially earn higher returns over the long term. It's important to understand the risks and seek professional advice if needed.

**Optimize Tax Strategies:**

Understanding and utilizing tax strategies can maximize savings and reduce tax liabilities. Contributing to tax-advantaged accounts, such as health savings accounts (HSAs), flexible spending accounts (FSAs), or education savings accounts (ESAs), can provide tax benefits. Taking advantage of tax deductions, credits, and exemptions can further optimize tax savings.

**Review and Adjust Savings Strategy:**

Regularly reviewing and adjusting the savings strategy is crucial. Individuals should reassess their savings goals, financial situation, and progress periodically. Life circumstances change, and financial goals may evolve. It's important to ensure that the savings strategy remains aligned with current needs and objectives. Adjustments may include increasing the savings rate, reallocating funds to different goals, or exploring new investment opportunities.

**Cultivate a Mindset of Abundance:**

Developing a mindset of abundance rather than scarcity can positively impact savings. Embracing gratitude for what one already has and focusing on the possibilities for growth and abundance helps foster a positive financial outlook. This mindset shift encourages individuals to make choices aligned with their long-term financial well-being and prioritize saving for future goals.

**Conclusion:**

By implementing these saving strategies, individuals can optimize their financial growth and build a solid foundation for their future. Setting clear savings goals, creating a budget, automating savings, tracking and reducing expenses, practicing frugality, minimizing debt, maximizing retirement contributions, exploring high-yield savings accounts and investments, optimizing tax strategies, reviewing and adjusting the savings strategy, and cultivating a mindset of abundance are all key components. With dedication, discipline, and a long-term perspective, individuals can achieve financial security and reach their savings goals. Remember, financial growth is a journey, and every step towards saving is a step closer to financial freedom.

## 2.3  Effective Debt Management

Debt is a common financial tool that allows individuals to make significant purchases or invest in opportunities. However, if not managed properly, debt can become burdensome and hinder financial progress. Effective debt management is crucial for achieving financial stability, reducing stress, and creating a solid foundation for long-term financial success. In this chapter, we will explore various strategies and techniques to manage debt effectively and regain control over your financial situation.

**Understand Your Debt:**

The first step in effective debt management is to understand your debt. Compile a list of all your debts, including credit card balances, student loans, personal loans, and mortgages. Note the outstanding balances, interest rates, minimum payments, and repayment terms for each debt. This comprehensive overview will provide a clear picture of your overall debt situation.

**Develop a Debt Repayment Strategy:**

Creating a debt repayment strategy is essential for managing debt effectively. There are two common approaches: the snowball method and the avalanche method.

- **Snowball Method:** Start by paying off the debt with the smallest balance while making minimum payments on other debts. Once the smallest debt is paid off, redirect the money towards the next smallest debt. This method provides a psychological boost as debts are eliminated one by one.

- **Avalanche Method:** Focus on paying off the debt with the highest interest rate while making minimum payments on other debts. Once the highest-interest debt is paid off, move on to the debt with the next highest interest rate. This method minimizes the overall interest paid over time.

Choose the method that aligns best with your preferences and financial situation. The key is to remain consistent and committed to your debt repayment strategy.

**Create a Budget:**

Developing a budget is crucial for effective debt management. Analyze your income and expenses, and create a detailed budget that allows for debt repayment while covering necessary living expenses. Identify areas where you can reduce spending to free up additional funds for debt repayment. Stick to your budget and track your progress regularly.

**Minimize New Debt:**

To effectively manage your existing debt, it is essential to minimize new debt. Avoid unnecessary purchases or using credit cards for discretionary spending. If possible, pay for expenses in cash or use a debit card to prevent adding to your debt load. Make a conscious effort to live within your means and prioritize your debt repayment goals.

**Negotiate Lower Interest Rates:**

High-interest rates can significantly impact your ability to repay your debt. Consider negotiating with your creditors or lenders to lower the interest rates on your loans or credit cards. Explain your financial situation and demonstrate your commitment to repaying the debt. Lowering the interest rate can save you money over the long term and expedite your debt repayment progress.

**Consolidate or Refinance Debt:**

Debt consolidation or refinancing can be beneficial for managing multiple debts and simplifying repayment. Consolidating your debts involves combining multiple debts into a single loan, often with a lower interest rate.

This simplifies the repayment process and may reduce the total monthly payment. Refinancing entails replacing an existing loan with a new one that offers more favorable terms, such as a lower interest rate or extended repayment period.

**Seek Professional Advice:**

If managing your debt becomes overwhelming or complex, consider seeking professional advice from a credit counselor or a debt management agency. These professionals specialize in helping individuals develop customized debt management plans. They can provide expert guidance on budgeting, debt consolidation, negotiation with creditors, and developing strategies to repay debt efficiently. A professional can also provide emotional support and motivation during challenging times.

**Prioritize High-Interest Debt:**

To effectively manage your debt, prioritize paying off high-interest debt first. High-interest debt, such as credit card debt, accumulates more interest over time, making it costlier to repay. Allocate a larger portion of your available funds towards these high-interest debts while making minimum payments on lower-interest debts. By targeting high-interest debt, you can reduce the overall interest expenses and accelerate your debt repayment progress.

**Increase Your Income:**

Increasing your income can provide additional resources to manage and repay your debt. Explore opportunities for a salary increase in your current job or consider taking up a side gig or part-time work. The extra income can be directly allocated towards debt repayment, allowing you to pay off your debts more quickly. Use this additional income strategically and resist the temptation to increase your spending.

**Communicate with Creditors:**

If you're experiencing financial hardship or struggling to make payments, it's important to communicate with your creditors. Ignoring their calls or letters will not make the debt disappear and can lead to further complications. Reach out to your creditors and explain your situation honestly. They may be willing to work with you to create a modified payment plan or provide temporary relief until your financial situation improves. Open communication can help prevent penalties, late fees, or negative impacts on your credit score.

**Cut Expenses:**

Reducing your expenses is an effective way to free up more money for debt repayment. Review your budget and identify areas where you can cut back on nonessential spending. Evaluate your monthly subscriptions, dining out habits, entertainment expenses, and discretionary purchases. Consider downsizing your living arrangements, exploring more affordable transportation options, or reducing utility costs. Every dollar saved can be directed towards paying down your debt.

**Stay Motivated and Track Progress:**

Managing debt requires discipline and perseverance. Stay motivated by setting milestones and celebrating small victories along the way. Track your progress regularly to see how far you've come. Consider using debt tracking tools or apps that visualize your debt repayment journey. Seeing the decreasing balances and increasing progress can provide the motivation to stay committed to your debt management plan.

**Focus on Financial Education:**

Invest in your financial education to improve your understanding of debt management and personal finance. Read books, attend workshops, or take online courses to enhance your knowledge of budgeting, debt management strategies, and financial planning. The more informed you are, the better equipped you'll be to make sound financial decisions and effectively manage your debt.

## Conclusion:

Effectively managing debt requires a combination of discipline, strategic planning, and perseverance. By understanding your debt, creating a budget, developing a debt repayment strategy, minimizing new debt, and seeking professional advice when necessary, you can take control of your financial situation. Remember to prioritize high-interest debt, increase your income if possible, communicate with creditors, cut expenses, and stay motivated along your debt repayment journey. With a proactive approach and commitment to your financial well-being, you can successfully manage your debt and pave the way towards a debt-free future.

## 2.4 Maximizing Credit Score and Reducing Interest Payments

Your credit score plays a vital role in your financial well-being. It affects your ability to secure loans, obtain favorable interest rates, and access financial opportunities. Additionally, reducing interest payments can save you significant money over time. In this chapter, we will explore strategies to maximize your credit score and reduce interest payments, helping you achieve better financial stability and save money in the long run.

**Part 1: Maximizing Credit Score**

**Understand Credit Scores:**

To maximize your credit score, it's crucial to understand how credit scores are calculated. The most commonly used scoring model is the FICO score, which considers factors such as payment history, credit utilization, length of credit history, credit mix, and new credit. Educate yourself about these factors and their impact on your credit score.

**Monitor Your Credit Report:**

Regularly monitoring your credit report allows you to identify any errors or discrepancies that may be negatively impacting your credit score. Obtain free copies of your credit report from the major credit bureaus (Equifax, Experian, and TransUnion) annually and review them carefully. If you find any inaccuracies, dispute them with the credit bureaus to have them corrected.

**Pay Bills on Time:**

Payment history is a significant factor in determining your credit score. Paying your bills on time is crucial to maintaining a good credit score. Set up automatic payments or reminders to ensure you never miss a payment. Late payments can have a detrimental impact on your credit score, so strive to make timely payments consistently.

**Reduce Credit Utilization:**

Credit utilization refers to the percentage of your available credit that you are currently using. Keeping your credit utilization ratio low is beneficial for your credit score. Aim to keep your utilization below 30% of your total available credit. Paying down debts and avoiding maxing out credit cards can help reduce your credit utilization ratio.

**Increase Credit Limits:**

Another way to lower your credit utilization ratio is by increasing your credit limits. Contact your credit card issuers and request a credit limit increase. This can help improve your credit utilization ratio as long as you don't increase your spending to match the higher limit. However, exercise caution to avoid accumulating more debt.

**Maintain a Mix of Credit Types:**

Having a healthy mix of credit types can positively impact your credit score. Lenders prefer to see a mix of revolving credit (such as credit cards) and instalments loans (such as a mortgage or auto loan). However, avoid opening new accounts solely to improve your credit mix, as this can negatively impact your credit score in the short term.

**Avoid Closing Old Credit Accounts:**

Closing old credit accounts can potentially harm your credit score. Length of credit history is an important factor, so keeping older accounts open demonstrates a longer credit history. If you no longer use a credit card, consider keeping it open and using it occasionally to keep it active.

**Use Credit Responsibly:**

Using credit responsibly is crucial for maintaining a good credit score. Avoid taking on excessive debt, applying for multiple credit cards or loans within a short period, and making unnecessary credit

# 3. Chapter 3

## The Art of Investing

To convert $100 into $1,000,000, you must manage your finances wisely. Start by creating a budget that outlines your income, expenses, and savings goals. Identify areas where you can reduce unnecessary spending and allocate those funds towards savings and investments.

### 3.1    Understanding Different Investment Vehicles

Investing is a key component of financial planning and wealth building. There are various investment vehicles available, each with its own characteristics, risks, and potential returns. Understanding different investment vehicles is crucial for making informed investment decisions and achieving your financial goals. In this chapter, we will explore some of the most common investment vehicles, including stocks, bonds, mutual funds, exchange-traded funds (ETFs), and real estate.

**Stocks:**

Stocks represent ownership shares in a company. When you buy stocks, you become a shareholder and have a claim on the company's assets and earnings. Stocks offer the potential for capital appreciation and dividends. They can be categorized into different types, including common stocks and preferred stocks. Common stocks typically offer voting rights and higher potential returns but also come with higher risks. Preferred stocks provide a fixed dividend but usually have limited voting rights.

**Bonds:**

Bonds are debt instruments issued by governments, municipalities, and corporations to raise capital. When you buy a bond, you are essentially lending money to the issuer in exchange for regular interest payments and the return of the principal at maturity. Bonds are generally considered less risky than stocks but offer lower potential returns. They can be further classified based on the issuer, such as government bonds, municipal bonds, and corporate bonds. Government bonds are considered the least risky as they are backed by the full faith and credit of the government.

**Mutual Funds:**

Mutual funds pool money from multiple investors to invest in a diversified portfolio of stocks, bonds, or other securities. They are managed by professional fund managers who make investment decisions on behalf of the investors. Mutual funds provide diversification and convenience, making them suitable for investors with different risk tolerances and investment goals. They can be categorized into different types, including equity funds, bond funds, index funds, and sector funds. Investors buy shares in the mutual fund, and the value of their investment is determined by the fund's net asset value (NAV).

### Exchange-Traded Funds (ETFs):

ETFs are similar to mutual funds in that they pool money from multiple investors to invest in a diversified portfolio of securities. However, unlike mutual funds, ETFs trade on stock exchanges like individual stocks. ETFs can track specific market indexes or be actively managed. They offer flexibility, liquidity, and transparency to investors. Investors buy and sell ETF shares on the stock exchange at market prices, which may be different from the underlying net asset value.

### Real Estate:

Real estate is an investment vehicle that involves purchasing and owning properties for potential appreciation and rental income. Real estate can include residential properties, commercial properties, or even real estate investment trusts (REITs), which are companies that own and manage income-generating real estate properties. Real estate investments can provide a steady stream of income and the potential for long-term capital appreciation. However, they require careful evaluation, market research, and property management.

### Other Investment Vehicles:

Apart from stocks, bonds, mutual funds, ETFs, and real estate, there are other investment vehicles worth mentioning. These include:

### Options and Futures:

These are derivative instruments that give investors the right to buy or sell an asset at a predetermined price and date. They are more complex and often used by sophisticated investors for hedging or speculative purposes.

### Commodities:

Commodities are physical goods such as gold, oil, or agricultural products. Investors can trade commodities through futures contracts or invest in commodity-based mutual funds or ETFs.

### Certificates of Deposit (CDs):

CDs are time deposits offered by banks with a fixed interest rate and maturity date. They are considered low-risk investments and provide a guaranteed return of principal.

**Precious Metals:**

Precious metals like gold, silver, and platinum can be purchased as an investment to hedge against inflation or economic uncertainty. They can be held physically or invested in through specialized funds or ETFs.

Understanding different investment vehicles is essential for building a well-diversified investment portfolio and achieving your financial goals. Stocks offer potential growth and ownership in companies, while bonds provide fixed income and lower risk. Mutual funds and ETFs provide diversification and professional management. Real estate offers income and potential appreciation. Other investment vehicles, such as options, futures, commodities, CDs, and precious metals, provide additional investment opportunities. It's important to consider your risk tolerance, investment goals, time horizon, and liquidity needs when choosing the appropriate investment vehicles. Diversification and regular review of your investment portfolio are key to managing risk and maximizing returns. Remember to conduct thorough research or seek professional advice before making any investment decisions.

Here are a few additional investment vehicles that are worth mentioning:

### Index Funds:

Index funds are a type of mutual fund or ETF that aims to replicate the performance of a specific market index, such as the S&P 500. They offer broad market exposure, low costs, and a passive investment approach. Index funds are a popular choice for investors seeking diversification and long-term growth.

### Retirement Accounts:

Retirement accounts, such as Individual Retirement Accounts (IRAs) and employer-sponsored plans like 401(k)s or 403(b)s, provide tax advantages for long-term savings. These accounts offer various investment options, including stocks, bonds, mutual funds, and target-date funds. Investing in retirement accounts allows individuals to grow their savings while potentially benefiting from tax deferral or tax-free growth.

### Peer-to-Peer Lending:

Peer-to-peer lending platforms connect borrowers directly with investors. Investors can lend money to individuals or small businesses and earn interest on their investment. This alternative investment vehicle can offer potentially higher returns compared to traditional fixed-income investments, but it also carries higher risks.

### Hedge Funds:

Hedge funds are private investment funds that cater to high-net-worth individuals and institutional investors. They employ sophisticated strategies, such as leveraging, short-selling, and derivatives, with the aim of generating higher returns. Hedge funds typically have high minimum investment requirements and are subject to less regulatory oversight.

**Venture Capital:**

Venture capital involves investing in early-stage or high-growth companies with the potential for significant returns. Venture capitalists provide funding to startups in exchange for equity ownership. This investment vehicle requires careful evaluation of business models, market potential, and management teams. Venture capital investments are typically illiquid and carry a higher level of risk.

**Cryptocurrencies:**

Cryptocurrencies, such as Bitcoin and Ethereum, have gained popularity in recent years. They are digital assets that use cryptography for secure transactions. Investing in cryptocurrencies can offer high potential returns, but it also comes with high volatility and regulatory risks. It's important to thoroughly research and understand the risks associated with this investment vehicle.

While stocks, bonds, mutual funds, ETFs, and real estate are among the most common investment vehicles, there are several other options available for investors. Index funds, retirement accounts, peer-to-peer lending, hedge funds, venture capital, and cryptocurrencies provide alternative avenues for diversifying investment portfolios and potentially generating higher returns. It's essential to assess your risk tolerance, investment objectives, and time horizon before deciding on the appropriate investment vehicles. Diversification and regular portfolio review are key to managing risk and optimizing returns. Consider consulting with a financial advisor or conducting thorough research to ensure informed investment decisions.

## 3.2    Developing an Investment Strategy

Developing a well-defined investment strategy is essential for achieving long-term financial goals, managing risk, and maximizing returns. An investment strategy serves as a roadmap to guide your investment decisions and actions. It considers your risk tolerance, financial goals, time horizon, and market conditions. In this chapter, we will explore the key components of developing an effective investment strategy.

**Define Your Financial Goals:**

The first step in developing an investment strategy is to define your financial goals. Are you investing for retirement, purchasing a home, funding your children's education, or achieving financial independence? Clearly articulate your short-term and long-term financial goals, along with the timeframes for achieving them. This will help determine your investment horizon and risk tolerance.

**Assess Your Risk Tolerance:**

Understanding your risk tolerance is crucial in designing an investment strategy that aligns with your comfort level. Risk tolerance refers to the degree of volatility and potential loss you are willing to accept in pursuit of higher returns. Consider factors such as your age, investment experience, income stability, and financial obligations. A risk tolerance questionnaire or consultation with a financial advisor can provide further insights into your risk profile.

**Determine Your Investment Horizon:**

Your investment horizon is the length of time you plan to hold your investments. It can range from short-term (less than 3 years) to intermediate-term (3-10 years) or long-term (10 years or more). Longer investment horizons generally allow for a higher allocation to growth-oriented investments, while shorter horizons may necessitate a more conservative approach. Consider the time remaining until you need to access your funds to tailor your investment strategy accordingly.

**Asset Allocation:**

Asset allocation is the process of distributing your investment portfolio across different asset classes, such as stocks, bonds, and cash equivalents. It is a crucial component of an investment strategy as it determines your exposure to different risk levels and potential returns. The allocation should be based on your financial goals, risk tolerance, investment horizon, and market conditions. Generally, younger investors with longer time horizons can have a higher allocation to equities for potential growth, while older investors may lean towards a more conservative allocation.

### Diversification:

Diversification is a risk management technique that involves spreading your investments across different securities, sectors, and geographical regions. By diversifying your portfolio, you reduce the impact of any single investment's performance on your overall portfolio. Diversification helps mitigate risk and increase the potential for consistent returns. Allocate your investments across various asset classes, industries, and regions to minimize exposure to specific risks.

### Investment Selection:

Once you have determined your asset allocation and diversification strategy, the next step is selecting specific investments within each asset class. This can include individual stocks, bonds, mutual funds, ETFs, or other investment vehicles. Conduct thorough research, analyze historical performance, assess risk factors, and consider factors such as fees, expenses, and liquidity. Consider your investment goals, time horizon, and risk tolerance when making investment selections.

### Regular Monitoring and Review:

An investment strategy is not a set-it-and-forget-it plan. Regular monitoring and review are essential to ensure your investments remain aligned with your strategy and goals. Review your portfolio periodically, analyze performance, and make adjustments as needed.

Changes in market conditions, economic factors, or personal circumstances may warrant a reallocation of assets or adjustments to your investment strategy.

**Cost Considerations:**

Consider the costs associated with your investments, such as management fees, commissions, and expense ratios. Higher costs can erode investment returns over time. Look for low-cost investment options, such as index funds or ETFs, which offer broad market exposure at lower expenses. Consider the trade-offs between cost and potential returns when selecting investment vehicles.

**Rebalancing:**

Rebalancing involves periodically adjusting your investment portfolio back to its original asset allocation targets. Market fluctuations can cause your portfolio to deviate from your desired allocation. Rebalancing allows you to sell overperforming assets and purchase underperforming assets, effectively buying low and selling high. Set specific thresholds or a regular schedule for rebalancing to maintain your desired asset allocation.

**Emotion Management:**

Emotions can influence investment decisions and lead to irrational behavior. Fear and greed can prompt investors to buy or sell at the wrong time, potentially hurting their investment returns. Develop strategies to manage your emotions, such as staying informed, maintaining a long-term perspective, and avoiding impulsive decisions based on short-term market fluctuations.

**Seek Professional Advice:**

Consider consulting with a financial advisor or investment professional to help develop and fine-tune your investment strategy. An experienced advisor can provide valuable insights, help align your strategy with your goals, and provide guidance during market fluctuations. They can also assist with portfolio monitoring, rebalancing, and adjustments based on changing circumstances.

**Conclusion:**

Developing an investment strategy is a crucial step in achieving your financial goals and building long-term wealth. By defining your financial goals, assessing your risk tolerance, determining your investment horizon, establishing an asset allocation and diversification plan, selecting appropriate investments, regularly monitoring and reviewing your portfolio, considering costs, rebalancing periodically, managing emotions, and seeking professional advice, you can create a robust investment strategy. Remember that investing is a long-term endeavor, and adjustments may be needed along the way. Stay informed, remain disciplined, and stay focused on your financial goals to maximize the potential for investment success.

### 3.3 Building a Diversified Portfolio

Building a diversified portfolio is a fundamental principle of successful investing. A diversified portfolio helps manage risk, maximize returns, and protect against potential losses. It involves spreading investments across different asset classes, industries, regions, and investment styles. In this chapter, we will explore the importance of diversification and the key considerations for building a diversified portfolio.

**Why Diversification Matters:**

Diversification is essential for managing risk. By investing in a variety of assets, you reduce the impact of any single investment on your overall portfolio. Different investments tend to perform differently under various market conditions. When one investment is experiencing a downturn, another may be performing well, helping to balance out the overall portfolio performance. Diversification can provide more stable returns over the long term and reduce the potential for significant losses.

**Asset Classes:**

Building a diversified portfolio starts with allocating investments across different asset classes. Common asset classes include stocks, bonds, cash equivalents, and alternative investments. Each asset class has its own risk and return characteristics. Stocks offer potential for capital appreciation but come with higher volatility. Bonds provide fixed income but offer lower potential returns. Cash equivalents, such as money market funds, provide stability but minimal growth potential. Alternative investments, like real estate or commodities, can provide further diversification.

**Allocation:**

Determining the allocation of your portfolio among different asset classes is a crucial step. The allocation should align with your risk tolerance, investment goals, and time horizon. Generally, younger investors with longer time horizons can have a higher allocation to equities for potential growth. As investors approach retirement or have shorter time horizons, they may shift towards a more conservative allocation with a higher proportion of bonds and cash equivalents.

**Geographic Diversification:**

Geographic diversification involves investing in different regions and countries. Economic conditions, regulatory environments, and market cycles can vary across regions. By investing globally, you reduce the risk of being overly exposed to a single country's economic or political events. Consider diversifying investments among developed markets, emerging markets, and international markets to gain exposure to different economies and industries.

**Industry Diversification:**

Diversifying across industries helps mitigate the risk of overconcentration in a single sector. Industries perform differently based on various factors, including market conditions, consumer trends, and technological advancements. Allocating investments across different industries, such as technology, healthcare, finance, and consumer goods, ensures that your portfolio is not overly dependent on the performance of a single sector.

**Company Size and Style Diversification:**

Diversifying investments across different company sizes and investment styles is important. Large-cap, mid-cap, and small-cap stocks each have unique risk and return characteristics. Large-cap stocks are typically more stable, while small-cap stocks may offer greater growth potential but with higher volatility. Similarly, growth stocks and value stocks have different investment characteristics. Allocating investments across different company sizes and investment styles helps balance risk and potential returns.

**Mutual Funds and ETFs:**

Mutual funds and exchange-traded funds (ETFs) can be valuable tools for diversification. These investment vehicles pool money from multiple investors and invest in a diversified portfolio of securities. They provide exposure to a broad range of assets within a specific asset class, industry, or region. By investing in mutual funds or ETFs, you can achieve instant diversification without having to purchase individual securities.

**Rebalancing:**

Rebalancing is the process of adjusting your portfolio back to its original asset allocation targets. Market fluctuations can cause the portfolio to deviate from the desired allocation. Rebalancing involves selling overperforming assets and purchasing underperforming assets to bring the portfolio back in line with the desired allocation. Regular rebalancing helps maintain diversification and ensures that your portfolio aligns with your investment strategy.

**Risk Management:**

Diversification is an effective risk management technique. However, it's important to note that diversification does not eliminate all risk. It helps manage risk by spreading investments across different assets, but it does not guarantee a profit or protect against losses. It's crucial to assess the risk and potential rewards of each investment and ensure that the overall risk profile of the portfolio aligns with your risk tolerance.

### Ongoing Monitoring and Adjustments:

Building a diversified portfolio is not a one-time task. Regular monitoring and adjustments are essential. Keep track of your investments, assess their performance, and stay informed about market conditions and economic trends. Reassess your asset allocation periodically and make adjustments as necessary based on changes in your risk tolerance, investment goals, or market conditions.

### Dollar-Cost Averaging:

Implementing a dollar-cost averaging strategy can help smooth out market volatility. Instead of investing a lump sum at once, regularly invest a fixed amount at predetermined intervals. This approach reduces the risk of making poor investment timing decisions and allows you to buy more shares when prices are low and fewer shares when prices are high.

### Consider Risk Factors:

While diversification helps manage risk, it's important to consider other risk factors such as interest rate risk, inflation risk, and currency risk. Allocate investments across different asset classes that have varying risk exposures to mitigate the impact of specific risks on your portfolio.

**Consider Investment Correlations:**

Understand the correlations between different investments in your portfolio. Investments that have a low or negative correlation can provide additional diversification benefits. When one investment performs poorly, others with low correlations may offset the losses, reducing overall portfolio volatility.

**Review Fees and Expenses:**

Pay attention to the fees and expenses associated with your investments. High fees can eat into your returns over time. Consider low-cost investment options such as index funds or ETFs that offer broad market exposure at lower expenses.

**Stay Informed and Educated:**

Continuously educate yourself about investing and stay informed about market trends, economic indicators, and changes in regulations. This knowledge will help you make informed decisions, assess risks, and identify potential opportunities for diversification.

**Embrace a Long-Term Perspective:**

Diversification is a long-term strategy. It's important to maintain a disciplined approach and avoid making knee-jerk reactions based on short-term market fluctuations. Stick to your investment strategy and be patient, allowing time for the benefits of diversification to compound over the long term.

**Seek Professional Advice if Needed:**

Building a diversified portfolio can be complex, and professional financial advice can provide valuable insights and guidance. Consider consulting with a financial advisor or investment professional to help design and monitor your portfolio, especially if you have specific investment goals or complex financial circumstances.

**Conclusion:**

Building a diversified portfolio is a key component of successful investing. By allocating investments across different asset classes, regions, industries, and investment styles, you can manage risk, maximize returns, and protect against potential losses. Consider your risk tolerance, investment goals, and time horizon when determining your asset allocation. Regularly monitor and rebalance your portfolio to maintain diversification. Remember that diversification does not eliminate all risk, and it's important to conduct thorough research or seek professional advice before making investment decisions. Building a well-diversified portfolio takes time, discipline, and ongoing evaluation, but it provides a solid foundation for long-term investment success.


## 3.4    Evaluating Risk and Reward

Evaluating the risk and reward of an investment is a critical aspect of making informed financial decisions. The risk-reward relationship assesses the potential for gaining or losing value in an investment compared to the level of risk involved. Understanding the interplay between risk and reward is essential for developing a well-balanced investment strategy. In this chapter, we will explore the factors to consider when evaluating risk and reward and how to strike a balance between the two.

**Understanding Risk:**

Risk refers to the uncertainty or potential for loss associated with an investment. Different investments carry varying levels of risk, and it's important to assess and understand these risks before committing capital. Here are some key types of risk to consider:

**Market Risk:**

Market risk refers to the potential for investments to be affected by overall market conditions. Factors such as economic trends, geopolitical events, or changes in interest rates can impact the value of investments.

### Credit Risk:

Credit risk is the risk of default by a borrower or issuer of debt securities. It includes the potential for non-payment of interest or principal on bonds or loans. Evaluating the creditworthiness of issuers is crucial when assessing credit risk.

### Liquidity Risk:

Liquidity risk arises when there is a lack of buyers or sellers for a particular investment, making it difficult to buy or sell without impacting the price. Investments with lower liquidity may have higher transaction costs or limited access to funds when needed.

### Concentration Risk:

Concentration risk occurs when a portfolio is heavily weighted towards a particular investment, sector, or geographic region. Overexposure to a single asset or market segment increases the potential impact of negative events on the overall portfolio.

### Assessing Potential Rewards:

Reward refers to the potential return or gain an investment can generate. Different investments offer varying levels of potential rewards. It's important to evaluate the potential rewards in relation to the risks involved.

Here are some key factors to consider when assessing potential rewards:

## Historical Performance:

Reviewing the historical performance of an investment can provide insights into its potential rewards. Analyze past returns over different time periods and compare them to relevant benchmarks or industry averages.

## Fundamental Analysis:

Conducting fundamental analysis involves assessing the financial health, growth prospects, and competitive position of the underlying asset or company. This analysis can help estimate the potential for future earnings or income and inform expectations for potential rewards.

## Yield or Return:

Evaluate the yield or return potential of an investment. For example, bonds provide fixed interest payments, while stocks may offer dividends and capital appreciation. Real estate investments may generate rental income and property value appreciation. Consider the income and growth potential of the investment.

### Investment Time Horizon:

Consider the investment time horizon and align it with the potential rewards. Some investments, such as long-term stocks, may offer higher potential returns but with increased short-term volatility. Shorter-term investments may provide lower returns but greater stability.

### Risk-Reward Trade-Off:

The risk-reward trade-off involves finding a balance between the potential for higher returns and the associated level of risk. Here are some key considerations when striking the right balance:

### Risk Tolerance:

Assess your risk tolerance, which is your ability and willingness to endure potential investment losses. Investors with a higher risk tolerance may be more comfortable with investments that have higher potential rewards but also higher volatility.

### Time Horizon:

Consider your investment time horizon. Longer-term investments may have higher potential rewards, but shorter-term investments may offer greater liquidity and lower volatility. Align your investment horizon with your risk profile and financial goals.

**Diversification:**

Diversifying your portfolio across different asset classes, industries, and regions can help manage risk and potentially enhance rewards. Diversification spreads risk and reduces the impact of a single investment on the overall portfolio.

**Risk Management Strategies:**

Implement risk management strategies such as stop-loss orders or setting asset allocation targets. These strategies can help limit losses and protect gains by automatically adjusting investment positions based on predetermined thresholds.

**Professional Advice:**

Consider seeking professional advice from a financial advisor or investment professional. They can help assess your risk tolerance, understand your financial goals, and provide guidance on balancing risk and reward within your investment strategy.

**Regular Monitoring and Adjustments:**

Evaluating risk and reward is an ongoing process. Markets, economic conditions, and investment landscapes change over time. Regularly monitor your investments, review their performance, and assess whether the risk and potential rewards are aligning with your expectations and goals. Adjust your portfolio as needed to maintain a balance between risk and reward based on changes in market conditions or your personal circumstances.

**Education and Research:**

Investing in your own financial knowledge is crucial for evaluating risk and reward effectively. Continuously educate yourself on investment principles, financial markets, and investment vehicles. Conduct thorough research on individual investments, review company financial statements, and analyse industry trends. Stay informed about economic indicators and geopolitical events that may impact investments.

**Conclusion:**

Evaluating risk and reward is an essential aspect of making informed investment decisions. Understanding the types of risks associated with an investment and assessing potential rewards are crucial for striking the right balance. Consider market risk, credit risk, liquidity risk, and concentration risk when evaluating risk. Assess historical performance, fundamental analysis, yield, and investment time horizon when assessing potential rewards. The risk-reward trade-off involves finding a balance that aligns with your risk tolerance, investment goals, and time horizon. Diversification, risk management strategies, professional advice, and ongoing monitoring are key components of evaluating risk and reward. Continuously educate yourself and conduct thorough research to make informed investment decisions. Remember that risk and reward are interconnected, and there are no guarantees in investing. By carefully evaluating risk and potential rewards, you can make informed decisions and build a well-balanced investment portfolio.

# 4. The Power of Passive Income

Passive income is a type of income that is generated with minimal effort or direct involvement on an ongoing basis. It is income earned from sources such as rental properties, dividends, interest, royalties, and businesses that operate without requiring active participation. Passive income has the potential to provide financial freedom, flexibility, and the ability to build wealth. In this chapter, we will explore the power of passive income and how it can transform your financial situation.

## 4.1    Unleashing the Potential of Passive Income

Passive income is a powerful concept that has the potential to transform your financial situation and provide greater freedom and flexibility in your life. Unlike active income, which requires trading time for money, passive income allows you to earn money with minimal ongoing effort. In this chapter, we will explore how to unleash the potential of passive income and take steps towards achieving financial independence and creating a life of abundance.

**Embrace the Mindset of Passive Income:**

To unleash the potential of passive income, it is crucial to adopt the right mindset. Understand that building passive income streams requires upfront effort and dedication, but it can lead to long-term rewards. Embrace the idea of creating assets that generate income and focus on developing a passive income mindset that prioritizes financial freedom, wealth creation, and the pursuit of opportunities beyond traditional employment.

**Identify and Evaluate Passive Income Opportunities:**

The first step in unleashing the potential of passive income is to identify and evaluate various opportunities. Consider different sources of passive income, such as real estate investments, dividend-paying stocks, peer-to-peer lending, royalties from intellectual property, or creating an online business. Evaluate each opportunity based on factors like income potential, risk level, required initial investment, and your personal interests and skills.

**Start with a Solid Foundation:**

Building passive income requires a solid foundation. Assess your current financial situation and make efforts to improve it. Reduce debt, save money, and establish an emergency fund. Strengthen your financial position to have a stable base from which to invest and generate passive income. Having a strong foundation will provide you with more flexibility and confidence as you embark on your passive income journey.

**Invest in Income-Generating Assets:**

To create passive income, invest in income-generating assets that have the potential to generate ongoing cash flow. Real estate properties, such as rental properties or real estate investment trusts (REITs), can provide rental income. Dividend-paying stocks can offer regular dividend payments. Peer-to-peer lending platforms allow you to lend money and earn interest. Carefully research and analyse each investment opportunity to ensure it aligns with your risk tolerance and financial goals.

**Build a Diverse Portfolio:**

Diversification is key to unleashing the potential of passive income. Avoid relying on a single income stream and instead build a diverse portfolio of passive income sources. Allocate investments across different asset classes, industries, and geographic regions to spread risk. A diverse portfolio can provide stability, protect against downturns in specific sectors, and increase the overall income potential.

**Passive Business Ventures:**

Consider starting a passive business venture that generates income without requiring your constant presence or active management. This could involve creating an online store, developing an app, or launching a website that generates revenue through advertising or affiliate marketing. Automation and outsourcing can play a significant role in running these businesses, allowing you to generate income while minimizing direct involvement.

**Continuously Educate Yourself:**

Unleashing the potential of passive income requires ongoing learning and education. Stay informed about investment strategies, market trends, and new opportunities. Read books, attend seminars, and engage with like-minded individuals who are pursuing passive income. Continuous learning will help you adapt to changing market conditions, make informed investment decisions, and identify new income-generating opportunities.

**Reinvest and Scale:**

As your passive income streams start generating cash flow, reinvest a portion of the income to scale your passive income endeavours. This could involve acquiring additional income-generating assets, expanding your business ventures, or exploring new investment opportunities. Reinvesting and scaling can accelerate your passive income growth and increase the potential for higher returns over time.

**Monitor and Adjust:**

Regularly monitor the performance of your passive income streams and make necessary adjustments.

Assess the income generated, evaluate the return on investment, and analyse any changes in market conditions. Adjust your portfolio or business strategies as needed to optimize income generation and minimize risks. Continuously evaluate the performance of your passive income sources and seek ways to improve and optimize your overall income portfolio.

**Embrace Patience and Persistence:**

Unleashing the potential of passive income is not an overnight process. It requires patience, persistence, and a long-term perspective. Building passive income streams takes time and effort. Be prepared for challenges, setbacks, and the need to adapt to changing circumstances. Embrace a mindset of perseverance and stay focused on your long-term financial goals.

**Conclusion:**

Unleashing the potential of passive income can provide you with financial freedom, flexibility, and the opportunity to create wealth. By adopting the right mindset, identifying and evaluating passive income opportunities, building a diverse portfolio, investing in income-generating assets, starting passive business ventures, continuously educating yourself, reinvesting and scaling, monitoring and adjusting, and embracing patience and persistence, you can embark on a journey towards financial independence and a life of abundance.

Remember that unleashing the potential of passive income requires dedication, ongoing learning, and adaptability. Stay committed to your goals and take action to unlock the power of passive income in your life.

## 4.2 Real Estate Investments and Rental Income

Real estate investments offer the potential for generating passive income through rental properties. Investing in real estate can provide a steady cash flow, long-term appreciation, and diversification in your investment portfolio. In this chapter, we will explore the benefits and considerations of real estate investments and how rental income can become a valuable source of passive income.

**Benefits of Real Estate Investments:**

Real estate investments offer several advantages that make them attractive for generating passive income:

**Cash Flow:**

Rental properties can generate regular cash flow through rental income. This cash flow can provide a consistent source of passive income, helping to cover property expenses, mortgage payments, and potentially yielding additional profit.

**Appreciation:**

Real estate has the potential to appreciate in value over time. As property values increase, the equity in your investment grows, providing the opportunity for capital appreciation and potential wealth accumulation.

**Diversification:**

Real estate investments can provide diversification in your investment portfolio. Real estate is an asset class that tends to have a low correlation with stocks and bonds, reducing the overall risk of your investment portfolio.

**Tax Advantages:**

Real estate investments offer various tax benefits. These can include deductions for mortgage interest, property taxes, depreciation, and operating expenses. Consult with a tax professional to understand the specific tax advantages available to you.

**Inflation Hedge:**

Real estate investments can act as a hedge against inflation. Rental income and property values have the potential to increase in line with inflation, helping to preserve your purchasing power over the long term.

**Types of Real Estate Investments:**

There are various types of real estate investments to consider when seeking rental income:

### Residential Properties:

Residential properties, such as single-family homes, townhouses, or condominiums, are popular choices for real estate investors. They offer the advantage of being in high demand for rental purposes and provide the opportunity for steady rental income.

### Multi-Family Properties:

Multi-family properties, such as apartment buildings or duplexes, can provide multiple rental units, increasing the potential for higher rental income. However, managing multi-family properties may require additional effort and expertise.

### Commercial Properties:

Commercial properties, including office buildings, retail spaces, or industrial warehouses, can offer higher rental rates and longer lease terms. Commercial properties often require a deeper understanding of the market and tenant needs.

### Vacation Rentals:

Vacation rentals, such as beachfront properties or cabins, can provide rental income during peak travel seasons. However, they may have higher vacancy rates during off-peak periods and require active management to handle bookings and maintenance.

**Considerations for Real Estate Investments:**

Before investing in real estate for rental income, consider the following factors:

**Location:**

The location of the property plays a crucial role in its rental potential. Look for properties in areas with strong rental demand, good infrastructure, amenities, and potential for future growth. Research the local market and understand rental trends and vacancy rates.

**Property Management:**

Determine whether you will manage the property yourself or hire a property management company. Property management involves tasks such as finding tenants, collecting rent, handling maintenance issues, and ensuring compliance with local regulations. Outsourcing property management can provide convenience but comes with associated costs.

**Financing:**

Consider your financing options for acquiring the property. Evaluate the down payment requirements, interest rates, and loan terms. A strong credit history and a favourable debt-to-income ratio can improve your chances of securing favourable financing options.

**Cash Flow Analysis:**

Conduct a cash flow analysis to evaluate the potential profitability of the investment. Consider expenses such as mortgage payments, property taxes, insurance, maintenance costs, and vacancies. Compare these expenses to the expected rental income to determine the net cash flow generated by the property.

**Tenant Screening:**

Proper tenant screening is essential for minimizing the risk of late payments or property damage. Perform background checks, verify income and employment, and request references to ensure reliable and responsible tenants.

**Property Maintenance and Upkeep:**

Maintaining the property is crucial for attracting and retaining tenants and ensuring a steady rental income stream. Regularly inspect the property, address maintenance issues promptly, and allocate a portion of rental income for ongoing repairs and renovations. Well-maintained properties tend to command higher rental rates and attract quality tenants.

**Rental Market Trends and Adjustments:**

Stay informed about rental market trends and adjust rental rates accordingly. Monitor local rental market conditions, vacancy rates, and rental rates for comparable properties. Regularly review and adjust rental rates to ensure they remain competitive and in line with market demands.

**Long-Term Appreciation:**

While rental income is a primary focus, real estate investments also have the potential for long-term appreciation. As property values increase over time, your investment can grow in value, offering the potential for significant capital appreciation. However, it's important to note that real estate markets can be cyclical, and property values can fluctuate. Maintain a long-term perspective and be prepared for market fluctuations.

**Risks and Mitigation:**

Real estate investments come with risks that should be carefully considered:

**Market Risk:**

Real estate values can be influenced by market conditions, economic factors, and local supply and demand dynamics. Conduct thorough market research and consider long-term trends when assessing market risks.

**Cash Flow Risks:**

Vacancies, late payments, or unexpected repairs can impact cash flow. Plan for contingencies by maintaining an emergency fund and conducting regular property inspections.

**Regulatory Risks:**

Stay informed about local regulations and comply with landlord-tenant laws, building codes, and zoning regulations. Failure to comply with regulations can result in legal and financial consequences.

**Financing Risks:**

If you finance the property, consider interest rate fluctuations and the impact they may have on mortgage payments. Ensure you have a sustainable cash flow even if interest rates increase.

**Property Management Risks:**

If you choose to manage the property yourself, be prepared for the responsibilities and challenges that come with it. Property management requires time, effort, and knowledge of legal and financial aspects.

**Conclusion:**

Real estate investments can provide a powerful source of passive income through rental properties. With careful evaluation, proper management, and an understanding of market dynamics, real estate investments have the potential to generate steady rental income, long-term appreciation, and diversification in your investment portfolio. Consider factors such as property location, financing options, property management, cash flow analysis, tenant screening, and property maintenance when investing in rental properties. Remember to conduct thorough due diligence, stay informed about market trends, and assess the risks involved. By strategically investing in real estate and leveraging rental income, you can build a solid foundation for passive income and financial growth.

## 4.3 Dividend Investing and Stock Market Returns

Dividend investing is a strategy that focuses on investing in stocks that pay regular dividends to shareholders. Dividends are a portion of a company's earnings distributed to its shareholders as a reward for their investment. Dividend investing can provide investors with not only a steady income stream but also the potential for capital appreciation through stock market returns. In this chapter, we will explore the concept of dividend investing, its benefits, and how it can contribute to overall stock market returns.

**Understanding Dividend Investing:**

Dividend investing involves investing in companies that have a history of paying consistent dividends. These companies are typically mature, established, and have a stable cash flow. Dividends can be paid on a quarterly, semi-annual, or annual basis, providing investors with a regular income stream. Dividend investing is particularly appealing to income-focused investors seeking a reliable source of passive income.

**Benefits of Dividend Investing:**

Dividend investing offers several benefits that contribute to overall stock market returns:

**Income Generation:**

Dividend-paying stocks provide investors with a regular stream of income. This income can supplement other sources of income and provide stability during market downturns or periods of low capital appreciation.

**Dividend Growth:**

Some companies increase their dividends over time, allowing investors to benefit from growing income. Dividend growth can outpace inflation and contribute to long-term wealth accumulation.

**Capital Appreciation:**

Dividend-paying stocks can also provide capital appreciation as their stock prices increase over time. Investors can benefit from both the income generated by dividends and the potential for stock price appreciation.

**Risk Mitigation:**

Dividend-paying stocks tend to be more stable and less volatile than non-dividend-paying stocks. The regular income provided by dividends can help mitigate the impact of market fluctuations and reduce portfolio risk.

**Compounding Effect:**

Reinvesting dividends can lead to the compounding effect, where dividend income is reinvested to purchase more shares. Over time, this can significantly enhance overall stock market returns.

**Dividend Metrics:**

When evaluating dividend-paying stocks, it is important to consider several key metrics:

**Dividend Yield:**

Dividend yield is the annual dividend payment divided by the stock price. It represents the percentage return an investor can expect from dividends alone. A higher dividend yield may indicate a more attractive investment, but it is important to consider other factors as well.

**Dividend Payout Ratio:**

The dividend payout ratio is the percentage of a company's earnings paid out as dividends. A lower payout ratio suggests that a company has more room to increase dividends in the future or reinvest earnings for growth.

**Dividend History:**

Assess the company's dividend history to determine its consistency and reliability in paying dividends. Look for a track record of stable or growing dividends over multiple years.

### Dividend Sustainability:

Consider the company's financial health and ability to sustain dividend payments. Evaluate factors such as cash flow, earnings growth, debt levels, and industry dynamics to ensure the company can continue paying dividends in the future.

### Reinvesting Dividends:

Reinvesting dividends is a powerful strategy to enhance overall stock market returns. Instead of taking dividend payments as cash, investors can choose to reinvest them by purchasing additional shares of the dividend-paying stock. Reinvesting dividends allows for compounding growth, as the additional shares generate their own dividends, which are subsequently reinvested. Over time, this compounding effect can significantly increase the total return on the investment.

### Risks and Considerations:

While dividend investing offers several advantages, it is important to be aware of potential risks and considerations:

### Dividend Cuts:

Companies may reduce or eliminate their dividends due to financial challenges or changes in their business environment. Research the financial health of companies and monitor any signs of potential dividend cuts.

### Market Risks:

Dividend-paying stocks are still subject to overall market risks. Economic downturns, industry-specific challenges, and market volatility can impact the stock prices of dividend-paying companies.

### Sector Concentration:

Be mindful of over-concentration in specific sectors or industries. Diversify your dividend portfolio across different sectors to mitigate the risk of sector-specific challenges.

### Dividend Taxation:

Dividends may be subject to taxation, depending on the tax laws of your jurisdiction. Consult with a tax professional to understand the tax implications of dividend income and optimize your tax strategy.

### Building a Dividend Portfolio:

Building a dividend portfolio involves selecting a diverse range of dividend-paying stocks across different sectors. Consider companies with a history of consistent dividend payments, strong financials, and potential for future growth. A well-diversified dividend portfolio can provide a balanced mix of income, stability, and potential for capital appreciation.

### Monitoring and Adjusting:

Regularly monitor your dividend portfolio and adjust your holdings as needed. Keep track of dividend payments, dividend growth rates, and any changes in a company's financial situation or industry dynamics. Stay informed about market trends, economic indicators, and company-specific news that may impact the performance of dividend-paying stocks.

### Seeking Professional Advice:

Consider seeking professional advice from a financial advisor or investment professional with expertise in dividend investing. They can help assess your financial goals, risk tolerance, and time horizon, and provide guidance on building and managing a dividend portfolio that aligns with your investment objectives.

### Conclusion:

Dividend investing offers investors the opportunity to generate regular income while potentially benefiting from capital appreciation. Dividend-paying stocks can contribute to overall stock market returns through the combination of dividend income and the potential for stock price appreciation. The benefits of dividend investing include income generation, dividend growth, risk mitigation, and the compounding effect of reinvesting dividends. However, it is important to consider dividend metrics, such as dividend yield and payout ratio, as well as the financial health and sustainability of companies. Monitor your dividend portfolio regularly, diversify across sectors, and be aware of potential risks and market fluctuations. With careful evaluation, dividend investing can be a powerful strategy to enhance overall stock market returns and build long-term wealth.

## 4.4     Creating Digital Products and Online Business

In the digital age, creating digital products and establishing an online business has become an increasingly popular and lucrative avenue for entrepreneurship. Digital products offer the advantage of scalability, low production costs, and the potential to reach a global audience. In this chapter, we will explore the process of creating digital products, the benefits of starting an online business, and the key considerations for success in the digital marketplace.

**Understanding Digital Products:**

Digital products are intangible goods or services that can be created, distributed, and consumed digitally. They can take various forms, such as e-books, online courses, software applications, music, videos, graphics, templates, and more. Digital products offer numerous advantages over physical products, including ease of distribution, cost-effectiveness, and the potential for automated sales and delivery.

**Identifying Your Niche and Target Audience:**

To create successful digital products and establish an online business, it is crucial to identify your niche and target audience. Conduct market research to understand the needs, desires, and pain points of your target audience. Determine how your expertise, skills, or passion align with a specific market segment, and identify opportunities for creating digital products that cater to their needs.

**Creating High-Quality Digital Products:**

Creating high-quality digital products is essential for building credibility, attracting customers, and generating sales. Consider the following steps when creating digital products:

**Define Your Value Proposition:**

Clearly articulate the unique value and benefits your digital product offers to customers. Identify the problem it solves or the value it adds to their lives.

**Plan Your Content:**

Outline the structure and content of your digital product. Break it down into manageable sections or modules and ensure that it flows logically and effectively conveys the intended message or knowledge.

**Develop Engaging Content:**

Create content that is engaging, informative, and valuable to your target audience. Incorporate multimedia elements such as videos, images, and interactive features to enhance the learning or user experience.

### Focus on User Experience:

Pay attention to the user experience of your digital product. Make it easy to navigate, visually appealing, and user-friendly. Test your product with a sample audience to gather feedback and make improvements.

### Use Professional Tools:

Invest in professional tools and software to create and design your digital products. Utilize tools for content creation, graphic design, video editing, and website development to ensure a polished and professional end product.

### Establishing an Online Presence:

To sell your digital products and build an online business, you need to establish a strong online presence. Here are key steps to consider:

### Create a Website:

Develop a professional website that showcases your digital products, provides information about your business, and enables customers to make purchases or inquiries. Ensure your website is mobile-friendly and optimized for search engines.

### Content Marketing:

Develop a content marketing strategy to attract and engage your target audience. Create relevant and valuable content through blog posts, videos, podcasts, or social media. Share your expertise, address customer pain points, and establish yourself as a trusted authority in your niche.

### Search Engine Optimization (SEO):

Optimize your website and content for search engines to improve your online visibility. Research and implement relevant keywords, optimize meta tags and descriptions, and create quality backlinks to increase organic traffic to your website.

### Social Media Marketing:

Leverage social media platforms to promote your digital products and engage with your audience. Create profiles on platforms that align with your target audience, share valuable content, and actively engage with your followers.

### Email Marketing:

Build an email list by offering valuable content or incentives in exchange for visitors' email addresses. Utilize email marketing to nurture relationships with potential customers, provide updates about your products, and offer exclusive discounts or promotions.

### Pricing and Monetization Strategies:

Determining the right pricing and monetization strategy for your digital products is crucial. Consider factors such as production costs, market demand, perceived value, and competition. Common monetization strategies include:

### One-time Purchase:

Set a fixed price for customers to purchase your digital product as a one-time transaction. This approach works well for standalone products such as e-books or templates.

### Subscriptions or Memberships:

Offer recurring subscriptions or memberships for access to ongoing content, updates, or exclusive benefits. This model works well for online courses or membership communities.

### Upselling and Cross-selling:

Consider offering additional products or upgrades to customers who have already purchased your digital product. This can include advanced versions, supplementary materials, or related products.

### Affiliate Marketing:

Collaborate with other businesses or influencers in your niche to promote and sell your digital products in exchange for a commission. This can help expand your reach and attract new customers.

**Building Customer Relationships and Support:**

Building strong customer relationships and providing excellent customer support is essential for the success of your online business. Foster open communication, promptly respond to inquiries, and address customer concerns or feedback. Provide clear instructions on how to use your digital products and offer ongoing support or resources to enhance the customer experience.

**Continuous Improvement and Adaptation:**

The digital marketplace is dynamic and constantly evolving. To stay competitive, it is important to continuously improve and adapt your digital products and online business. Monitor customer feedback, analyze sales data, and stay informed about industry trends. Regularly update and enhance your digital products to meet changing customer needs and preferences.

**Protecting Intellectual Property:**

When creating and selling digital products, it is crucial to protect your intellectual property. Consider copyrighting your content, utilizing digital rights management (DRM) techniques, and including clear terms of use or licensing agreements. Consult with legal professionals to ensure your intellectual property is adequately protected.

**Conclusion:**

Creating digital products and establishing an online business can be a rewarding and profitable venture. By identifying your niche, creating high-quality digital products, building an online presence, utilizing effective pricing and monetization strategies, fostering customer relationships, and continuously improving your offerings, you can harness the power of the digital marketplace. Embrace the opportunities that digital products and online businesses offer, and leverage technology to reach a global audience and create a sustainable source of income in the digital age.

# 5. Entrepreneurship and Business Ventures

Entrepreneurship is the process of creating and managing a business venture with the aim of achieving profitability and growth. It involves taking calculated risks, identifying opportunities, and mobilizing resources to bring innovative ideas to fruition. Entrepreneurship is a dynamic and challenging journey that requires vision, determination, and a willingness to embrace uncertainty. In this chapter, we will explore the concept of entrepreneurship, the characteristics of successful entrepreneurs, and key considerations when starting a business venture.

## 5.1 Identifying Profitable Business Opportunities

Identifying profitable business opportunities is a crucial step in entrepreneurship. It involves recognizing market needs, analysing industry trends, and identifying gaps or underserved areas where a business can offer value and generate sustainable profits. In this chapter, we will explore the process of identifying profitable business opportunities and key factors to consider when evaluating their potential for success.

**Conduct Market Research:**

Market research is a vital component of identifying profitable business opportunities. It involves gathering information about the target market, industry trends, customer needs, and competitor analysis. Conduct the following market research activities:

### Identify Target Market:

Define your target market and understand its demographics, preferences, and behaviour. Determine the size of the market and its growth potential.

### Customer Analysis:

Conduct surveys, interviews, or focus groups to gain insights into customer needs, pain points, and preferences. Identify gaps or unmet needs that your business can address.

### Industry Analysis:

Evaluate industry trends, growth rates, and potential opportunities. Identify emerging markets, technological advancements, or regulatory changes that can impact your business.

### Competitor Analysis:

Analyse competitors' strengths, weaknesses, market share, pricing strategies, and customer value proposition. Identify areas where your business can differentiate itself and offer unique value.

### Identify and Validate Business Ideas:

Once you have conducted market research, brainstorm potential business ideas that align with market needs and your expertise. Validate these ideas by considering the following factors:

### Unique Value Proposition:

Assess the uniqueness and potential demand for your business idea. Determine how it addresses customer needs, solves a problem, or offers a competitive advantage over existing solutions.

### Feasibility:

Evaluate the feasibility of turning your business idea into a profitable venture. Consider factors such as resource availability, scalability, production costs, and technical requirements.

### Test Minimum Viable Product (MVP):

Develop a minimum viable product or prototype to test the market response. Gather feedback, iterate, and refine your product or service based on customer insights.

### Market Demand:

Assess the market demand for your product or service. Conduct surveys, test sales, or gather pre-orders to gauge customer interest and validate demand.

### Profitability Analysis:

Estimate the potential profitability of your business idea. Consider factors such as revenue streams, cost structure, pricing strategy, and projected financial performance.

### Evaluate Revenue Streams:

To identify profitable business opportunities, it is crucial to evaluate the revenue streams that your business can generate. Consider the following revenue models:

### Product Sales:

Generate revenue by selling physical or digital products to customers. Consider factors such as production costs, pricing strategies, distribution channels, and customer acquisition.

### Subscriptions or Memberships:

Offer recurring subscriptions or memberships to access your products or services. This model provides a predictable and recurring revenue stream.

### Licensing or Franchising:

License your intellectual property or business model to other companies or individuals in exchange for royalties or franchise fees.

### Advertising or Sponsorships:

Generate revenue by partnering with advertisers or sponsors who pay to promote their products or services to your target audience.

### Consulting or Services:

Offer specialized consulting or professional services to clients in your industry. This revenue model leverages your expertise and knowledge.

### Assess Market Competition:

Understanding the competitive landscape is crucial when evaluating business opportunities. Assess the competition by considering the following factors:

### Competitor Analysis:

Identify direct and indirect competitors in your industry. Analyse their products, pricing, marketing strategies, strengths, weaknesses, and customer perception.

### Differentiation:

Determine how your business can differentiate itself from competitors. Identify unique selling points, innovations, or superior customer experiences that set your business apart.

### Market Share:

Assess the market share held by competitors and evaluate their growth rates. Identify areas where your business can gain a competitive edge or target underserved market segments.

### Barriers to Entry:

Consider the barriers to entry in your industry. Evaluate factors such as capital requirements, regulations, intellectual property protection, and industry expertise.

### Market Saturation:

Determine if the market is saturated or if there is room for new entrants. Assess market demand and growth potential to ensure there is space for your business to thrive.

### Analyse Industry Trends:

Analysing industry trends is crucial for identifying profitable business opportunities. Consider the following factors:

### Technological Advancements:

Assess how technological advancements can disrupt or create new opportunities in your industry. Identify emerging technologies that can drive innovation and efficiency.

### Changing Consumer Behaviour:

Understand evolving consumer preferences, habits, and purchasing behaviour. Identify trends such as sustainability, digitalization, convenience, or personalized experiences.

### Economic and Socio-Cultural Factors:

Consider macroeconomic factors, demographic shifts, and socio-cultural trends that can impact consumer needs and preferences. Identify opportunities arising from these changes.

### Regulatory Environment:

Assess regulatory factors and changes that can impact your industry. Stay informed about industry-specific regulations, licensing requirements, or government incentives that can affect your business.

### Evaluate Operational and Financial Considerations:

To ensure profitability, evaluate operational and financial considerations of potential business opportunities:

### Cost Structure:

Assess the cost structure of your business, including production costs, overhead expenses, marketing expenses, and operational costs. Determine if the business can operate efficiently and generate profit margins.

### Scalability:

Evaluate the scalability of your business idea. Consider if it can be easily expanded to meet growing demand without incurring significant costs or operational challenges.

### Resource Requirements:

Determine the resources needed to start and run the business. Assess the availability and affordability of these resources, including physical infrastructure, technology, human capital, and funding.

### Return on Investment (ROI):

Estimate the potential return on investment for your business opportunity. Analyse the payback period, profitability ratios, and the potential for long-term sustainable growth.

### Cash Flow Management:

Evaluate the cash flow dynamics of your business. Consider factors such as sales cycles, payment terms, inventory management, and the ability to maintain positive cash flow.

**Risk Assessment:**

Identify potential risks and challenges associated with the business opportunity. Develop risk mitigation strategies and contingency plans to address these challenges.

**Conclusion:**

Identifying profitable business opportunities requires a thorough understanding of market needs, industry trends, competition, and operational considerations. Conducting comprehensive market research, validating business ideas, evaluating revenue streams, assessing market competition, analysing industry trends, and considering operational and financial factors are crucial steps in identifying profitable business opportunities. By carefully evaluating and selecting business ideas with high growth potential and profitability, entrepreneurs can increase their chances of building successful and sustainable ventures. However, it is important to continually adapt and refine strategies as market conditions change and new opportunities arise. With a keen eye for opportunities and a systematic approach to evaluation, entrepreneurs can identify and capitalize on profitable business opportunities.

## 5.2 Launching and Scaling a Startup

Launching and scaling a startup involves taking a business idea from concept to reality and growing it into a successful and sustainable venture. It is an exciting but challenging journey that requires careful planning, execution, and adaptability. In this chapter, we will explore the key steps involved in launching and scaling a startup, from ideation to growth strategies and scaling techniques.

**Ideation and Market Validation:**

The first step in launching a startup is generating a viable business idea and validating its potential in the market. Consider the following steps:

**Identify a Problem:**

Identify a problem or pain point that your startup aims to solve. Conduct market research, gather customer insights, and analyse industry trends to identify gaps or unmet needs.

**Develop a Value Proposition:**

Clearly define the unique value proposition of your startup. Identify how your product or service will address the identified problem and offer a compelling solution that differentiates you from competitors.

### Minimum Viable Product (MVP):

Develop a minimum viable product or prototype to test your idea in the market. Gather feedback from potential customers, iterate, and refine your product based on their needs and preferences.

### Market Validation:

Validate your business idea by obtaining early customer feedback and securing initial sales or commitments. This helps establish proof of concept and provides insights for further refinement.

### Creating a Business Plan:

Developing a comprehensive business plan is essential for outlining your startup's vision, objectives, and strategies. Consider the following elements:

### Executive Summary:

Provide a concise overview of your startup, its mission, and the problem it solves.

### Market Analysis:

Analyse the target market, industry trends, customer segments, and competitors. Identify your target audience and develop a marketing strategy.

**Product or Service Offering:**

Clearly define your product or service, its features, benefits, and unique selling points.

**Marketing and Sales Strategy:**

Outline your marketing and sales approach, including branding, pricing, distribution channels, and customer acquisition tactics.

**Operations and Resources:**

Define the operational processes, resources, and infrastructure required to deliver your product or service effectively.

**Financial Projections:**

Develop financial forecasts, including revenue projections, expense estimates, and cash flow analysis. Outline funding requirements and potential sources of investment.

**Building a Team:**

Assembling a capable and motivated team is crucial for startup success. Consider the following steps:

**Define Roles and Responsibilities:**

Clearly define roles and responsibilities within your startup. Identify the skills and expertise required for each role.

### Recruit Top Talent:

Attract and hire talented individuals who align with your startup's mission and culture. Utilize various recruitment channels, networks, and professional platforms.

### Foster a Positive Work Environment:

Create a supportive and inclusive work culture that fosters collaboration, innovation, and open communication.

### Provide Learning and Growth Opportunities:

Offer professional development opportunities, training programs, and mentorship to empower your team members to grow and thrive.

### Securing Funding:

Startups often require funding to fuel growth and development. Consider the following funding options:

### Bootstrapping:

Utilize personal savings, credit cards, or loans to self-fund your startup. This allows for greater control but may limit initial resources.

### Angel Investors:

Seek investment from angel investors who provide early-stage funding in exchange for equity. Angel investors often bring expertise, industry connections, and mentorship.

**Venture Capital:**

Approach venture capital firms for larger investments in exchange for equity. Venture capitalists often invest in high-growth startups with the potential for significant returns.

**Crowdfunding:**

Leverage crowdfunding platforms to raise funds from a large number of individuals who believe in your startup's vision. Offer rewards or equity in return for contributions.

**Government Grants and Programs:**

Research government grants, subsidies, or startup support programs that provide financial assistance to early-stage ventures.

**Marketing and Customer Acquisition:**

Developing effective marketing strategies and acquiring customers are crucial for startup growth. Consider the following steps:

**Identify Target Audience:**

Clearly define your target audience and create detailed customer personas. Understand their needs, preferences, and buying behaviour.

**Branding and Positioning:**

Develop a compelling brand identity and positioning that resonates with your target audience. Create a consistent brand message and visual identity across all marketing channels.

**Digital Marketing:**

Leverage digital marketing channels, such as social media, content marketing, search engine optimization (SEO), and pay-per-click (PPC) advertising, to reach your target audience cost-effectively.

**Partnerships and Influencer Marketing:**

Collaborate with complementary businesses or industry influencers to expand your reach and tap into their existing customer base.

**Customer Relationship Management:**

Build strong relationships with your customers through personalized communication, excellent customer support, and loyalty programs.

### Scaling and Growth Strategies:

Scaling a startup involves expanding operations, increasing market share, and achieving sustainable growth. Consider the following strategies:

### Product or Service Expansion:

Expand your product or service offerings to cater to a broader range of customer needs. Introduce new features, variations, or complementary offerings.

### Market Expansion:

Enter new geographic markets or target new customer segments to expand your customer base. Conduct market research to understand local preferences and adapt your marketing strategies accordingly.

### Strategic Partnerships:

Form strategic partnerships with other businesses to leverage their resources, expertise, and customer base. Explore joint ventures, distribution partnerships, or co-marketing initiatives.

### Technology Adoption:

Embrace technology to streamline operations, improve efficiency, and enhance the customer experience. Leverage automation, data analytics, and artificial intelligence to gain a competitive edge.

### Scalable Infrastructure:

Build a scalable infrastructure that can accommodate growth. Invest in robust systems, processes, and technologies that can handle increased demand and operational complexity.

### Talent Acquisition and Development:

Attract and retain top talent to support your growth initiatives. Continuously invest in the professional development of your team and foster a culture of innovation and learning.

### Continuous Innovation and Adaptation:

Innovation and adaptability are essential for long-term startup success. Consider the following:

### Continuous Improvement:

Continuously evaluate and improve your products, processes, and strategies. Solicit feedback from customers, track market trends, and iterate on your offerings to stay competitive.

### Embrace Change:

Embrace change and be open to pivoting your business model or strategies based on market feedback and evolving customer needs. Stay agile and adaptable to seize new opportunities.

**Foster a Culture of Innovation:**

Encourage innovation within your startup. Foster an environment where creativity and new ideas are valued. Empower your team members to experiment and take calculated risks.

**Stay Ahead of Trends:**

Stay informed about industry trends, emerging technologies, and market shifts. Proactively identify potential disruptions and capitalize on opportunities they present.

**Customer-Centric Approach:**

Put the customer at the centre of your decision-making processes. Listen to customer feedback, anticipate their evolving needs, and tailor your offerings accordingly.

**Conclusion:**

Launching and scaling a startup is a dynamic and challenging Endeavor. By following a structured approach, including ideation and market validation, creating a business plan, building a talented team, securing funding, implementing effective marketing strategies, and adopting growth-focused strategies, entrepreneurs can increase their chances of success. Continuous innovation, adaptability, and a customer-centric approach are crucial for sustaining growth and staying competitive in an ever-evolving business landscape. While the journey may be demanding, the rewards of successfully launching and scaling a startup can be immensely fulfilling both personally and financially.

## 5.3    Building a Successful Online Business

In today's digital era, building a successful online business has become increasingly accessible and lucrative. The internet offers vast opportunities to reach a global audience, automate processes, and create scalable business models. However, building a successful online business requires careful planning, execution, and adaptation to the ever-changing digital landscape. In this chapter, we will explore the key steps involved in building a successful online business and the essential factors to consider along the way.

**Define Your Business Idea and Target Market:**

The first step in building a successful online business is defining your business idea and identifying your target market. Consider the following steps:

**Identify Your Passion and Expertise:**

Start by identifying your passion and expertise. What are you genuinely interested in? What knowledge or skills do you possess that can be leveraged in an online business?

**Research Your Target Market:**

Conduct market research to identify your target audience. Understand their needs, preferences, and pain points. Analyse competitors to identify gaps or opportunities in the market.

**Develop Your Unique Selling Proposition:**

Define your unique selling proposition (USP). What sets your online business apart from competitors? What value or benefit will you provide to your target audience?

**Create a Compelling Brand Identity:**

Creating a compelling brand identity is essential for building trust, establishing credibility, and attracting customers. Consider the following steps:

**Define Your Brand Values:**

Determine the core values that your online business stands for. Clearly articulate your mission, vision, and brand personality.

**Develop a Memorable Brand Name and Logo:**

Create a unique and memorable brand name and design a visually appealing logo that represents your brand identity.

**Craft Your Brand Messaging:**

Develop clear and consistent brand messaging across all platforms. Clearly communicate your USP, value proposition, and the benefits customers can expect.

### Consistent Visual Identity:

Establish a consistent visual identity with a cohesive color scheme, typography, and design elements across your website, social media, and other marketing channels.

### Build an Engaging Website or Online Store:

Your website or online store serves as the virtual storefront for your online business. It should be visually appealing, user-friendly, and optimized for conversions. Consider the following steps:

### Choose a Reliable Web Hosting Platform:

Select a reliable web hosting platform that ensures your website's security, performance, and uptime.

### User Experience (UX) Design:

Prioritize user experience by designing a clean and intuitive website layout. Make it easy for visitors to navigate, find information, and make purchases.

### Mobile Responsiveness:

Ensure your website is mobile-responsive to provide a seamless browsing and shopping experience across various devices.

**Optimize for Search Engines:**

Implement search engine optimization (SEO) strategies to improve your website's visibility in search engine results. Research and incorporate relevant keywords, optimize meta tags, and create high-quality content.

**Secure Payment Gateways:**

Provide secure payment options for customers by integrating trusted payment gateways that protect sensitive information.

**Develop an Effective Marketing Strategy:**

To drive traffic, attract customers, and generate sales, a well-executed marketing strategy is crucial. Consider the following components:

**Content Marketing:**

Create valuable and relevant content such as blog posts, videos, infographics, or podcasts to engage your target audience. Share your expertise, address customer pain points, and build trust and credibility.

**Social Media Marketing:**

Leverage social media platforms where your target audience is active. Develop a social media strategy to share content, engage with followers, and build a community around your brand.

**Email Marketing:**

Build an email list and develop an email marketing strategy to nurture leads, promote your products or services, and drive repeat purchases.

**Pay-Per-Click (PPC) Advertising:**

Utilize PPC advertising platforms like Google Ads or social media advertising to reach a wider audience, increase brand visibility, and drive targeted traffic to your website.

**Influencer Marketing:**

Collaborate with influencers or industry experts who have a strong online presence and a relevant audience. Partner with them to promote your products or services and increase brand awareness.

**Search Engine Marketing (SEM):**

Implement paid search advertising campaigns to appear in search engine results for specific keywords related to your business.

**Prioritize Customer Experience and Support:**

Providing exceptional customer experience and support is crucial for building customer loyalty and repeat business. Consider the following steps:

**Prompt and Friendly Customer Support:**

Establish efficient customer support channels, such as email, live chat, or phone, to address customer inquiries, concerns, and provide assistance when needed.

**Personalization:**

Tailor your communication and marketing efforts to provide personalized experiences. Use customer data and segmentation to send targeted offers, recommendations, or personalized messages.

**Feedback and Reviews:**

Encourage customers to leave feedback and reviews about their experience with your online business. Monitor and respond to feedback to show that you value customer opinions.

**Seamless Ordering and Fulfillment:**

Streamline your ordering and fulfillment processes to ensure a seamless experience for customers. Provide accurate product information, transparent pricing, and reliable shipping options.

**Embrace Data Analytics and Optimization:**

Leveraging data analytics and optimization is essential for continuously improving your online business's performance and making informed decisions. Consider the following steps:

### Set Up Website Analytics:

Implement a robust web analytics tool, such as Google Analytics, to track and analyse website traffic, user behaviour, conversion rates, and other key performance indicators.

### Monitor Key Metrics:

Regularly monitor key metrics, such as traffic sources, bounce rates, conversion rates, and customer acquisition costs. Use these insights to identify areas for improvement and optimize your strategies.

### A/B Testing:

Conduct A/B testing to compare different versions of your website, landing pages, or marketing campaigns. Test different elements, such as headlines, call-to-action buttons, or pricing, to identify what resonates best with your audience.

### Conversion Rate Optimization (CRO):

Implement CRO techniques to optimize your website's conversion rates. Use data-driven insights to make incremental improvements to your website's design, layout, and messaging.

### Data-Driven Decision Making:

Make informed business decisions based on data analysis and insights. Use data to identify trends, customer preferences, and areas where you can optimize your marketing efforts.

**Adapt to Evolving Trends and Technologies:**

The digital landscape is constantly evolving, and staying ahead of the curve is crucial for the long-term success of your online business. Consider the following steps:

**Stay Updated on Industry Trends:**

Stay informed about industry trends, emerging technologies, and changes in consumer behaviour. Adapt your strategies and offerings to align with these trends.

**Embrace New Technologies:**

Embrace new technologies that can enhance your online business, such as artificial intelligence, chatbots, automation tools, or virtual reality. Evaluate how these technologies can improve efficiency, customer experience, and competitiveness.

**Continual Learning and Skill Development:**

Invest in continuous learning to stay up-to-date with digital marketing strategies, e-commerce trends, and technological advancements. Attend conferences, workshops, or online courses to expand your knowledge and skills.

**Conclusion:**

Building a successful online business requires a well-thought-out strategy, attention to detail, and a customer-centric approach. By defining your business idea, creating a compelling brand identity, building an engaging website, developing an effective marketing strategy, prioritizing customer experience, leveraging data analytics, and adapting to evolving trends, you can position your online business for success. Embrace the opportunities that the digital landscape offers, remain agile, and continuously optimize your strategies to meet the evolving needs of your target audience. With dedication, persistence, and the right approach, you can build a thriving online business that not only generates revenue but also provides value to your customers and contributes to your long-term success.

## 5.4 Effective Marketing and Sales Strategies

Effective marketing and sales strategies are essential for businesses to attract and retain customers, generate revenue, and achieve sustainable growth. In today's competitive landscape, businesses need to employ a mix of traditional and digital marketing tactics to reach their target audience, build brand awareness, and drive sales. In this chapter, we will explore key components of effective marketing and sales strategies and provide insights on how to implement them successfully.

**Understanding Your Target Audience:**

The first step in developing effective marketing and sales strategies is to understand your target audience. Consider the following steps:

**Define Buyer Personas:**

Create detailed buyer personas that represent your ideal customers. Consider demographics, psychographics, behaviours, and pain points.

**Conduct Market Research:**

Gather data and insights about your target market, including industry trends, customer preferences, and competitor analysis. This research will help you tailor your marketing messages and offerings.

### Identify Customer Needs:

Understand the needs and challenges of your target audience. Conduct surveys, interviews, or focus groups to gather feedback and uncover pain points that your products or services can address.

### Develop a Strong Brand Identity:

A strong brand identity helps differentiate your business from competitors and builds trust with your target audience. Consider the following steps:

### Brand Positioning:

Define your unique value proposition and how you want to be perceived in the market. Identify the key messages that resonate with your target audience.

### Visual Identity:

Develop a compelling visual identity, including a memorable logo, color scheme, typography, and consistent branding across all marketing materials.

### Brand Voice:

Establish a consistent brand voice that reflects your values and resonates with your target audience. Use this voice in all marketing communications to build brand recognition.

### Brand Storytelling:

Create compelling narratives that convey the mission, values, and personality of your brand. Use storytelling to engage and connect with your audience on an emotional level.

### Content Marketing:

Content marketing involves creating valuable and relevant content to attract, engage, and retain customers. Consider the following strategies:

### Blogging:

Develop a blog and regularly publish high-quality, informative content related to your industry. Address common pain points, share insights, and provide practical solutions.

### Social Media Content:

Create engaging content for social media platforms that aligns with your brand and resonates with your target audience. Use a mix of text, images, videos, and infographics.

### Video Marketing:

Utilize the power of video to showcase your products or services, share customer testimonials, or provide educational content. Videos can be shared on your website, social media platforms, or video hosting sites like YouTube.

### eBooks and Whitepapers:

Offer downloadable eBooks or whitepapers that provide in-depth information, guides, or research reports on topics of interest to your target audience. Use these resources to capture leads and demonstrate expertise.

### Webinars and Podcasts:

Host webinars or create podcasts to share industry insights, interviews with experts, or discussions on relevant topics. These formats allow for engagement and interactive communication.

### Search Engine Optimization (SEO):

SEO is crucial for improving your website's visibility in search engine results and driving organic traffic. Consider the following strategies:

### Keyword Research:

Identify relevant keywords that your target audience is searching for. Optimize your website's content, meta tags, headings, and URLs with these keywords.

**On-Page Optimization:**

Ensure that your website's pages are optimized for search engines. This includes optimizing title tags, meta descriptions, headers, and alt tags for images.

**Quality Content Creation:**

Develop high-quality, informative, and engaging content that is optimized for relevant keywords. Use internal and external links to enhance the credibility of your content.

**Technical SEO:**

Ensure that your website's technical aspects, such as site speed, mobile responsiveness, and URL structure, are optimized for search engines.

**Local SEO:**

If you have a physical location, optimize your website for local search queries by including location-specific keywords, creating local business listings, and obtaining positive customer reviews.

**Paid Advertising:**

Paid advertising allows businesses to reach a wider audience and drive targeted traffic to their websites. Consider the following advertising channels:

### Search Engine Marketing (SEM):

Run paid search ads on search engine platforms, such as Google Ads, to appear at the top of search results for relevant keywords. Set budgets, create compelling ad copy, and optimize your campaigns for maximum ROI.

### Display Advertising:

Utilize display ads on websites, mobile apps, and social media platforms to increase brand visibility and reach. Use visual elements and compelling messaging to capture the attention of your target audience.

### Social Media Advertising:

Leverage social media platforms like Facebook, Instagram, Twitter, and LinkedIn to run targeted ads. Define your audience, set budgets, and create visually appealing ads that align with each platform's best practices.

### Influencer Marketing:

Collaborate with influencers or industry experts who have a significant online following. Partner with them to promote your products or services and tap into their audience.

## Customer Relationship Management (CRM):

Effective customer relationship management is crucial for retaining customers and driving repeat business. Consider the following strategies:

### Customer Segmentation:

Segment your customer base based on demographics, purchase history, behaviour, or other relevant factors. This allows you to personalize your marketing messages and offerings.

### Email Marketing:

Develop targeted email campaigns to nurture leads, provide valuable content, and promote special offers or new products. Use marketing automation tools to streamline the process.

### Personalization:

Customize your communications and offers based on customer preferences, browsing history, or previous purchases. Provide personalized recommendations and exclusive discounts to enhance the customer experience.

### Customer Loyalty Programs:

Implement customer loyalty programs to reward repeat customers. Offer incentives such as discounts, exclusive access, or loyalty points that can be redeemed for future purchases.

### Customer Feedback and Support:

Encourage customer feedback and provide excellent customer support. Address inquiries promptly, resolve issues effectively, and actively seek feedback to improve your products or services.

### Sales Strategies:

Effective sales strategies help convert leads into customers and maximize revenue. Consider the following approaches:

### Sales Funnel Optimization:

Map out your sales funnel and identify areas where leads may drop off. Optimize each stage of the funnel to minimize friction and maximize conversions.

### Lead Generation:

Implement lead generation strategies, such as offering gated content, hosting webinars, or running targeted ads, to capture potential customers' contact information.

### Sales Collateral:

Develop sales collateral, such as sales decks, case studies, or product demos, that provide compelling information about your offerings and address customer pain points.

**Sales Team Training:**

Invest in training and development for your sales team. Equip them with product knowledge, effective communication skills, objection handling techniques, and negotiation strategies.

**Relationship Building:**

Foster strong relationships with customers through personalized interactions, follow-ups, and ongoing support. Focus on building trust, understanding customer needs, and delivering value.

**Upselling and Cross-Selling:**

Identify opportunities to upsell or cross-sell additional products or services to existing customers. Offer complementary or upgraded offerings based on their needs and preferences.

**Conclusion:**

Implementing effective marketing and sales strategies is crucial for businesses to succeed in today's competitive landscape. By understanding your target audience, developing a strong brand identity, creating valuable content, optimizing for search engines, utilizing paid advertising, nurturing customer relationships, and implementing effective sales strategies, you can attract and retain customers, generate revenue, and achieve sustainable growth. Continuously evaluate and adapt your strategies based on market trends, customer feedback, and performance metrics to ensure ongoing success in the dynamic business environment.

# 6. Embracing the Stock Market

The stock market is a dynamic and potentially rewarding avenue for individuals to grow their wealth and participate in the economy. It offers opportunities to invest in publicly traded companies and benefit from their growth and profitability. However, navigating the stock market requires knowledge, research, and a long-term perspective. In this chapter, we will explore the benefits of embracing the stock market and key considerations for successful investing.

## 6.1     Exploring Stock Market Investing

Stock market investing offers individuals the opportunity to participate in the growth and profitability of publicly traded companies. It can be a rewarding avenue for wealth creation and long-term financial growth. However, it is important to approach stock market investing with knowledge, research, and a long-term perspective. In this chapter, we will explore the key aspects of stock market investing, including understanding the stock market, assessing investment risks, conducting research, developing an investment strategy, and managing a stock portfolio.

**Understanding the Stock Market:**

The stock market is a platform where individuals and institutions buy and sell shares of publicly traded companies. It is a marketplace where buyers and sellers interact, determining the price and value of stocks. Understanding the following key concepts is essential:

**Stocks:**

Stocks represent ownership in a company. When individuals buy shares of a company's stock, they become shareholders and are entitled to a portion of the company's profits and assets.

**Stock Exchanges:**

Stock exchanges are centralized marketplaces where stocks are bought and sold. Examples include the New York Stock Exchange (NYSE) and NASDAQ.

**Stock Indices:**

Stock indices, such as the S&P 500 or Dow Jones Industrial Average, represent a basket of stocks that provide an overview of the overall market performance.

**Assessing Investment Risks:**

Before investing in the stock market, it is important to understand and assess the risks involved. Consider the following factors:

**Market Risk:**

Market fluctuations and volatility can impact stock prices. Factors such as economic conditions, political events, or industry trends can affect market performance.

**Company-Specific Risk:**

Each company has its own set of risks, including competition, regulatory changes, management quality, or financial health. Assessing these risks is crucial before investing.

**Diversification:**

Diversification is a risk management strategy that involves spreading investments across different stocks and sectors. It helps reduce the impact of individual company failures or sector-specific downturns.

**Risk Tolerance:**

Investors should assess their risk tolerance, which is the level of risk they are comfortable taking. It determines the investment strategy, asset allocation, and the ability to withstand market fluctuations.

**Conducting Research:**

Thorough research is essential for making informed investment decisions. Consider the following research methods:

### Fundamental Analysis:

This involves analysing a company's financial statements, such as its balance sheet, income statement, and cash flow statement. Assess key financial metrics, growth prospects, competitive advantages, and management quality.

### Technical Analysis:

Technical analysis involves studying stock price patterns and market trends using charts and statistical indicators. It helps identify buying and selling opportunities based on historical price and volume data.

### Company News and Reports:

Stay updated on company news, earnings reports, industry trends, and regulatory changes that may impact the stock's performance. Utilize financial news outlets, company websites, and research reports.

### Analyst Recommendations:

Analysts provide research reports and recommendations on stocks. Consider these recommendations as part of your research, but also conduct your own analysis.

**Developing an Investment Strategy:**

Developing a clear investment strategy helps guide your decision-making process. Consider the following elements:

**Investment Goals:**

Determine your investment goals, such as capital appreciation, dividend income, or long-term wealth accumulation. Define your time horizon and financial objectives.

**Asset Allocation:**

Decide on the allocation of your investment portfolio among different asset classes, such as stocks, bonds, and cash. Asset allocation should align with your risk tolerance and investment goals.

**Investment Style:**

Define your investment style, such as value investing, growth investing, or a combination of approaches. Each style has its own set of principles and strategies.

**Buy-and-Hold or Active Trading:**

Determine whether you prefer a buy-and-hold approach, where you hold stocks for the long term, or active trading, where you buy and sell stocks frequently based on short-term price movements.

### Regular Investing:

Consider implementing a regular investing plan, such as dollar-cost averaging. This involves investing a fixed amount at regular intervals, regardless of market conditions.

### Managing a Stock Portfolio:

Once you have invested in stocks, effective portfolio management is essential. Consider the following strategies:

### Monitor Your Portfolio:

Regularly review the performance of your stocks and the overall portfolio. Stay updated on company news, industry trends, and market conditions that may impact your investments.

### Rebalancing:

Rebalance your portfolio periodically to maintain your desired asset allocation. Sell stocks that have exceeded their target weight and buy stocks that have underperformed.

### Long-Term Perspective:

Stock market investing is a long-term endeavor. Avoid making hasty decisions based on short-term market fluctuations. Focus on the long-term prospects of the companies in your portfolio.

**Risk Management:**

Implement risk management strategies, such as using stop-loss orders or setting price targets for selling stocks. Regularly assess your portfolio's performance and adjust your investments as needed.

**Tax Considerations:**

Be mindful of the tax implications of your stock investments. Understand the tax rules related to capital gains, dividends, and any applicable deductions or exemptions.

**Professional Advice:**

Consider seeking professional advice from financial advisors or investment professionals who can provide personalized guidance based on your financial situation and investment goals.

**Conclusion:**

Embracing stock market investing offers individuals the opportunity to participate in the growth and profitability of publicly traded companies. By understanding the stock market, assessing investment risks, conducting thorough research, developing an investment strategy, and effectively managing a stock portfolio, investors can navigate the complexities of the market and increase their chances of achieving their financial goals. It is important to approach stock market investing with a long-term perspective, patience, and the willingness to continuously learn and adapt to changing market conditions.

## 6.2    Fundamental and Technical Analysis

Fundamental analysis and technical analysis are two distinct approaches used by investors to evaluate and make investment decisions in financial markets. While both approaches aim to assess the value of assets, they differ in the factors they consider and the methods they employ. In this chapter, we will explore fundamental analysis and technical analysis, their key principles, methodologies, and how they can be used to make informed investment decisions.

**Fundamental Analysis:**

Fundamental analysis is a method of evaluating the intrinsic value of an asset by examining its underlying factors and financial indicators. It focuses on understanding the business, industry, and economic factors that can impact the asset's value. Key components of fundamental analysis include:

**Financial Statements:**

Fundamental analysts analyse a company's financial statements, including the balance sheet, income statement, and cash flow statement. These statements provide insights into the company's financial health, profitability, and cash flow.

**Business Analysis:**

Fundamental analysts examine the company's business model, competitive advantages, growth prospects, and industry dynamics. They assess factors such as market share, customer base, product quality, management competency, and regulatory environment.

**Valuation Metrics:**

Fundamental analysis utilizes various valuation metrics, such as price-to-earnings (P/E) ratio, price-to-sales (P/S) ratio, price-to-book (P/B) ratio, and dividend yield. These metrics help determine if the asset is overvalued, undervalued, or fairly priced compared to its peers or historical averages.

**Economic Factors:**

Fundamental analysts consider macroeconomic factors, such as interest rates, inflation, GDP growth, and government policies, which can impact the overall economy and, subsequently, the performance of companies and industries.

**Industry Analysis:**

Fundamental analysts assess the industry dynamics and trends that can affect the company's growth and profitability. They consider factors such as competition, barriers to entry, technological advancements, and regulatory changes.

## Qualitative Factors:

Fundamental analysis incorporates qualitative factors, such as management integrity, corporate governance practices, brand reputation, and customer satisfaction. These factors can influence the company's long-term prospects and sustainability.

## Technical Analysis:

Technical analysis is a method of evaluating investments based on historical price and volume data, focusing on patterns, trends, and market psychology. It assumes that market prices reflect all available information and that historical patterns can help predict future price movements. Key components of technical analysis include:

## Price Charts:

Technical analysts analyse price charts to identify patterns, trends, support and resistance levels, and other technical indicators. Different types of charts, such as line charts, bar charts, and candlestick charts, are used to visualize price movements over time.

## Technical Indicators:

Technical analysis employs a wide range of indicators, such as moving averages, relative strength index (RSI), moving average convergence divergence (MACD), and stochastic oscillators. These indicators help identify potential entry and exit points based on price and volume patterns.

### Trend Analysis:

Technical analysts study trend lines, which connect successive highs or lows in price, to determine the direction of the market. They identify uptrends, downtrends, or sideways movements, and use this information to make buy or sell decisions.

### Support and Resistance Levels:

Technical analysts identify support levels (price levels where demand is expected to be strong) and resistance levels (price levels where supply is expected to be strong). These levels help determine potential entry and exit points.

### Volume Analysis:

Technical analysts analyse trading volume to gauge the strength of price movements. Higher volumes during price advances or declines are considered as confirmation of the trend.

### Chart Patterns:

Technical analysis identifies various chart patterns, such as head and shoulders, double tops, triangles, and flags. These patterns can indicate potential trend reversals or continuation.

**Market Sentiment:**

Technical analysts consider market sentiment and investor psychology. They examine indicators such as sentiment surveys, put/call ratios, and volatility indices to gauge market sentiment and potential shifts in investor behaviour.

**Application and Integration:**

While fundamental analysis and technical analysis are distinct approaches, many investors integrate elements from both to make well-rounded investment decisions. Here are a few ways in which they can be applied and integrated:

**Long-Term Investing:**

Fundamental analysis is typically used for long-term investing, as it focuses on the underlying value of assets. Investors analyse a company's financials, growth prospects, and industry dynamics to make informed investment decisions for the long run. However, technical analysis can still be used to identify favourable entry and exit points within a long-term investment strategy.

**Short-Term Trading:**

Technical analysis is commonly used by short-term traders who aim to profit from short-term price movements. Traders rely on chart patterns, technical indicators, and volume analysis to make quick buy or sell decisions. However, understanding the fundamentals of the underlying asset can provide additional insights and help mitigate risks.

**Risk Management:**

Fundamental analysis can provide a broader perspective on the risks and opportunities associated with an investment. It helps investors assess the financial health, competitive position, and growth potential of a company. Technical analysis, on the other hand, helps investors identify potential price levels for stop-loss orders or profit targets, thus managing risk on a trade-by-trade basis.

**Confirmation and Timing:**

Investors may use technical analysis to confirm their fundamental analysis. For example, they may wait for a technical indicator or a specific price pattern to align with their fundamental analysis before entering or exiting a position.

**Sector Rotation:**

Investors may use fundamental analysis to identify promising sectors or industries for long-term investment, and then use technical analysis to time their entry and exit points within those sectors.

**Conclusion:**

Fundamental analysis and technical analysis are two approaches that investors use to evaluate and make investment decisions in financial markets. Fundamental analysis focuses on assessing the intrinsic value of assets by analysing financial statements, business models, industry dynamics, and economic factors. Technical analysis, on the other hand, relies on historical price and volume data to identify patterns, trends, and market psychology.

Both approaches have their strengths and limitations, and investors often integrate elements from both to make well-rounded investment decisions. Fundamental analysis provides insights into the long-term value and prospects of an asset, while technical analysis helps identify short-term price movements and potential entry and exit points.

It is important to note that neither approach guarantees success in the stock market. Investors should consider their investment goals, risk tolerance, and time horizon when deciding which approach to use or how to integrate them. Additionally, ongoing learning, staying updated on market trends, and adapting strategies based on new information are essential for successful investing.

## 6.3　　Investing in Index Funds and ETFs

Investing in index funds and exchange-traded funds (ETFs) has gained popularity among investors seeking a diversified and low-cost approach to investing in the financial markets. These investment vehicles provide exposure to a broad range of assets, such as stocks, bonds, or commodities, while aiming to replicate the performance of a specific index. In this chapter, we will explore the benefits, considerations, and strategies involved in investing in index funds and ETFs.

**Understanding Index Funds and ETFs:**

**Index Funds:**

Index funds are mutual funds that aim to replicate the performance of a specific market index, such as the S&P 500 or the FTSE 100. They achieve this by holding a portfolio of securities that closely mirror the composition and weighting of the underlying index. Index funds are typically passively managed, meaning they do not involve active stock selection or market timing.

**Exchange-Traded Funds (ETFs):**

ETFs are investment funds that trade on stock exchanges, similar to individual stocks. Like index funds, ETFs aim to track the performance of an index, but they have additional flexibility in trading throughout the day.

ETFs can be passively managed, mirroring an index, or actively managed, where a fund manager makes investment decisions.

**Benefits of Investing in Index Funds and ETFs:**

**Diversification:**

Index funds and ETFs provide instant diversification by investing in a broad range of securities within a specific market or sector. This diversification helps spread risk across multiple companies, reducing the impact of individual stock price fluctuations.

**Low Costs:**

Index funds and ETFs are known for their relatively low expense ratios compared to actively managed funds. Since these funds aim to replicate the performance of an index, they do not require extensive research or active management, resulting in lower costs for investors.

**Transparency:**

Index funds and ETFs disclose their holdings regularly, allowing investors to know exactly what securities they own. This transparency helps investors understand the underlying assets and make informed investment decisions.

**Liquidity:**

ETFs trade on stock exchanges throughout the trading day, providing liquidity and flexibility for investors to buy or sell shares at market prices. This liquidity is advantageous for investors who prefer to actively manage their portfolios or adjust their positions based on market conditions.

**Tax Efficiency:**

Index funds and ETFs are generally tax-efficient investment vehicles. Due to their low turnover and passive management approach, they typically generate fewer taxable events, such as capital gains distributions, compared to actively managed funds.

Considerations When Investing in Index Funds and ETFs:

**Understanding the Index:**

Before investing in an index fund or ETF, it is important to understand the underlying index being tracked. Different indexes have different methodologies, sector allocations, and geographic exposures. Evaluating the index's historical performance, constituents, and correlation to your investment objectives is crucial.

**Expense Ratios and Fees:**

Although index funds and ETFs are known for their low costs, it is important to compare expense ratios and transaction fees among different funds. Small differences in expenses can significantly impact long-term returns.

**Tracking Error:**

While index funds and ETFs aim to replicate the performance of an index, there may be a slight deviation known as tracking error. Tracking error can result from factors such as fees, imperfect replication, or timing differences. Investors should assess the tracking error of the fund and evaluate its impact on performance.

**Market Volatility:**

Index funds and ETFs are subject to market volatility, as their performance closely mirrors the underlying index. During periods of market downturns or high volatility, these funds may experience temporary declines in value. Investors should have a long-term investment horizon and be prepared for short-term fluctuations.

**Strategies for Investing in Index Funds and ETFs:**

**Asset Allocation:**

Determine the appropriate asset allocation that aligns with your investment goals, risk tolerance, and time horizon. Index funds and ETFs can be used to represent various asset classes, such as domestic stocks, international stocks, bonds, or commodities, within your portfolio.

**Core-Satellite Approach:**

Employ a core-satellite approach by using index funds or ETFs as the core holdings in your portfolio, providing broad market exposure. Supplement this with satellite holdings of individual stocks or actively managed funds to achieve specific investment objectives or capture additional growth opportunities.

**Dollar-Cost Averaging:**

Consider implementing a dollar-cost averaging strategy by regularly investing a fixed amount in index funds or ETFs. This strategy involves buying more shares when prices are lower and fewer shares when prices are higher, potentially lowering the average cost per share over time.

**Rebalancing:**

Periodically review your portfolio's asset allocation and rebalance as needed. Rebalancing involves adjusting the portfolio's holdings back to the desired allocation, which helps maintain the desired risk profile and capture potential opportunities.

**Tax-Efficient Investing:**

In taxable accounts, consider tax-efficient investing strategies, such as utilizing tax-efficient index funds or ETFs that minimize capital gains distributions. Additionally, investors can strategically locate assets in taxable and tax-advantaged accounts to optimize tax efficiency.

**Conclusion:**

Investing in index funds and ETFs offers investors a diversified, low-cost, and transparent approach to participate in the financial markets. These investment vehicles provide instant diversification, liquidity, and the ability to track the performance of a specific index. By understanding the benefits, considering important factors, and employing appropriate investment strategies, investors can leverage index funds and ETFs to build well-rounded portfolios aligned with their investment goals and risk tolerance. As with any investment, thorough research, ongoing monitoring, and a long-term perspective are key to successful investing in index funds and ETFs.

## 6.4     Risk Management and Market Timing

Risk management and market timing are two important concepts in investing that aim to mitigate risks and enhance returns. Risk management involves strategies to identify, assess, and manage potential risks associated with investment decisions. Market timing, on the other hand, focuses on predicting market movements to determine the best times to enter or exit investment positions. In this chapter, we will explore the concepts of risk management and market timing, their significance in investing, and strategies for effectively incorporating them into investment decisions.

**Risk Management:**

Risk management is an essential aspect of investing that involves identifying, analysing, and mitigating potential risks. The goal is to protect capital and minimize potential losses while maximizing returns. Here are key components of risk management:

**Risk Assessment:**

Identify and assess various types of risks, including market risk, company-specific risk, industry risk, and liquidity risk. Evaluate the probability and potential impact of these risks on investment portfolios.

**Diversification:**

Diversify investments across different asset classes, sectors, geographic regions, and investment instruments to reduce the impact of individual investment risks. Diversification helps to spread risk and potentially enhance returns.

**Asset Allocation:**

Determine the appropriate asset allocation that aligns with your risk tolerance and investment goals. Balancing investments between stocks, bonds, cash, and other assets based on their risk-return profiles can help manage overall portfolio risk.

**Stop-Loss Orders:**

Implement stop-loss orders to automatically sell an investment if it reaches a predetermined price. This strategy can help limit potential losses by enforcing disciplined selling when the investment reaches a specified level of decline.

**Risk-Adjusted Returns:**

Evaluate investments based on their risk-adjusted returns, considering the level of risk taken to achieve those returns. Tools such as the Sharpe ratio or the sordino ratio can help assess an investment's performance relative to its risk.

**Regular Monitoring and Review:**

Continuously monitor the performance of investments, assess changing market conditions, and make adjustments to the portfolio as needed. Regular reviews help identify potential risks and opportunities and allow for timely risk management actions.

**Market Timing:**

Market timing refers to the strategy of predicting market movements and attempting to enter or exit investment positions based on these predictions. The goal is to buy investments at low prices and sell them at high prices. However, accurately timing the market consistently is challenging, and many studies suggest that market timing is difficult to achieve successfully. Here are key considerations related to market timing:

**Market Research and Analysis:**

Conduct thorough research and analysis of market trends, economic indicators, company fundamentals, and technical indicators to make informed investment decisions. Market timing often involves analysing multiple factors to assess the overall market direction.

**Contrarian Investing:**

Contrarian investors attempt to identify market turning points by taking positions opposite to prevailing market sentiment. They look for opportunities when market sentiment is overly pessimistic or optimistic, believing that markets tend to revert to their mean.

**Long-Term vs. Short-Term Perspective:**

Consider the investment horizon when making market timing decisions. Short-term market timing can be speculative and subject to higher risks, while long-term investing focuses on the fundamentals and potential growth of investments over an extended period.

**Cost of Market Timing:**

Frequent trading or attempting to time the market can result in higher transaction costs, including brokerage fees, taxes, and bid-ask spreads. These costs can erode potential gains and reduce overall portfolio returns.

**Potential Pitfalls:**

Market timing is challenging due to the unpredictable nature of markets, the impact of emotions, and the difficulty of consistently making accurate predictions. Mistiming the market can lead to missed opportunities or significant losses.

**Balancing Risk Management and Market Timing:**

While risk management and market timing are distinct concepts, they can be complementary in managing investment portfolios effectively. Here are strategies for balancing risk management and market timing:

**Long-Term Focus:**

Adopt a long-term investment approach focused on the fundamentals of investments and their potential for growth over time. Long-term investing reduces the emphasis on short-term market timing and allows for compounding returns.

**Systematic Investment:**

Implement a systematic investment plan, such as dollar-cost averaging, to invest a fixed amount at regular intervals. This strategy helps mitigate the impact of market timing by spreading investments over time.

**Strategic Asset Allocation:**

Develop a strategic asset allocation plan that aligns with your risk tolerance and investment goals. Regularly rebalance the portfolio to maintain the desired asset allocation, incorporating risk management principles.

**Fundamental Analysis:**

Focus on fundamental analysis to evaluate investments based on their financial health, growth prospects, competitive advantages, and industry dynamics. Fundamental analysis provides a long-term perspective and helps identify investments with strong underlying fundamentals.

**Risk Assessment and Mitigation:**

Continuously assess potential risks associated with investments and take appropriate risk management measures. Diversify investments, set stop-loss orders, and regularly review the portfolio to ensure risk exposure remains within acceptable levels.

**Patience and Discipline:**

Practice patience and discipline in investment decision-making. Avoid making impulsive decisions based on short-term market movements or emotions. Stick to the investment plan and maintain a long-term view.

**Conclusion:**

Risk management and market timing are important considerations in investing. Risk management involves identifying, assessing, and mitigating potential risks to protect capital and optimize returns. Market timing, on the other hand, focuses on predicting market movements to determine optimal entry and exit points for investments. While market timing can be challenging and difficult to consistently achieve, a balanced approach that incorporates risk management principles, long-term investing, systematic investment plans, strategic asset allocation, and fundamental analysis can help investors navigate the markets more effectively. Ultimately, investors should align their strategies with their risk tolerance, investment goals, and time horizon to achieve successful investment outcomes.

# 7. Real Estate Ventures

Real estate ventures involve investing in properties with the aim of generating income and potential appreciation over time. Real estate has long been considered a tangible and valuable asset class that offers various opportunities for investors. This chapter explores the key aspects of real estate ventures, including different investment strategies, types of properties, financing options, and considerations for successful real estate investing.

## 7.1    Introduction to Real Estate Investment

Real estate investment is the process of acquiring, owning, managing, and selling real estate properties with the goal of generating income and potential appreciation. Real estate has long been considered a tangible and valuable asset class that offers various opportunities for investors. It provides the potential for cash flow through rental income, long-term growth through property appreciation, and tax benefits. In this comprehensive guide, we will explore the key concepts, strategies, considerations, and steps involved in real estate investment.

**Benefits of Real Estate Investment:**

Real estate investment offers several benefits that make it an attractive option for investors:

**Cash Flow:**

Rental income from investment properties provides a steady cash flow stream, which can serve as a passive income source.

**Appreciation:**

Real estate properties have the potential to appreciate in value over time, allowing investors to benefit from capital appreciation.

**Diversification:**

Real estate investments can provide diversification to an investment portfolio, as they tend to have a low correlation with other asset classes, such as stocks and bonds.

**Inflation Hedge:**

Real estate investments have historically been considered a good hedge against inflation, as property values and rental income tend to rise with inflation.

**Tax Benefits:**

Real estate investors can benefit from various tax advantages, including deductions for mortgage interest, property taxes, depreciation, and 1031 exchanges for tax deferral.

**Types of Real Estate Investments:**

There are various types of real estate investments that investors can consider:

**Residential Properties:**

Residential properties include single-family homes, townhouses, condominiums, and multi-family properties. These properties are primarily used for residential purposes and can be rented out to tenants.

**Commercial Properties:**

Commercial properties include office buildings, retail spaces, industrial properties, and mixed-use properties. They are used for commercial purposes and offer potential for higher rental income.

**Real Estate Investment Trusts (REITs):**

REITs are investment vehicles that pool funds from multiple investors to invest in a portfolio of income-generating real estate properties. Investors can buy shares of publicly traded REITs, which provide an opportunity to invest in real estate without directly owning and managing properties.

**Real Estate Development:**

Real estate development involves acquiring land or existing properties and developing them for residential, commercial, or mixed-use purposes. This investment strategy requires expertise in development, construction, and project management.

### Setting Investment Goals and Strategy:

Before embarking on real estate investment, it is essential to define investment goals and develop a strategy:

### Investment Goals:

Determine your investment objectives, whether it's generating cash flow, achieving long-term appreciation, diversifying your portfolio, or building wealth for retirement. Clear goals will guide your investment decisions.

### Risk Assessment:

Evaluate your risk tolerance and understand the risks associated with real estate investment, such as market fluctuations, tenant vacancies, property maintenance, and financing risks.

### Investment Strategy:

Choose an investment strategy that aligns with your goals and risk tolerance. Common strategies include buy and hold, fix and flip, rental properties, real estate investment trusts (REITs), or a combination of strategies.

### Financial Considerations:

Assess your financial situation and determine the amount of capital you can allocate to real estate investments. Consider factors such as down payments, closing costs, property management expenses, and potential financing options.

### Market Analysis and Research:

Conducting market analysis and research is crucial for identifying favourable investment opportunities:

### Local Market Conditions:

Study the local real estate market to understand trends, supply and demand dynamics, population growth, job market, and rental market conditions. Analyse factors that can impact property values and rental income.

### Economic Factors:

Evaluate broader economic indicators, such as GDP growth, employment rates, interest rates, and inflation, as they can influence the overall real estate market.

### Property Demand and Supply:

Assess the demand and supply of properties in the market. Look for areas with strong demand, low vacancy rates, and limited supply to maximize rental income potential.

### Demographics and Trends:

Analyse demographic trends, such as population growth, age demographics, and migration patterns. Consider factors like proximity to schools, transportation, amenities, and emerging trends in real estate, such as sustainable and smart homes.

### Financing Real Estate Investments:

Real estate investments often require financing. Consider the following options:

### Conventional Mortgages:

Traditional bank mortgages are a common financing option for real estate investments. These loans typically require a down payment, have specific qualification criteria, and offer competitive interest rates.

### Private Financing:

Private lenders or individuals can provide financing options for real estate investments. These may include hard money loans, which offer shorter-term financing with higher interest rates and fewer qualification requirements.

### Seller Financing:

In some cases, sellers may be willing to finance a portion of the purchase price, allowing buyers to make payments directly to the seller over time.

**Real Estate Crowdfunding:**

Crowdfunding platforms allow investors to pool their capital with other investors to collectively invest in real estate projects. This option provides access to real estate investments with lower capital requirements.

**Property Selection and Analysis:**

Selecting the right property and conducting thorough analysis is critical for successful real estate investment:

**Criteria for Property Selection:**

Define your criteria for selecting properties, including location, property type, size, condition, potential for appreciation, rental demand, and cash flow potential.

**Property Analysis:**

Perform due diligence on properties of interest, including reviewing financials, property history, rent rolls, leases, and property condition reports. Analyse key metrics, such as cash-on-cash return, cap rate, and return on investment (ROI).

**Due Diligence Process:**

Conduct a comprehensive due diligence process, which may include property inspections, title searches, environmental assessments, and legal review. This process helps identify any potential issues or risks associated with the property.

### Property Valuation:

Utilize various property valuation methods, such as comparative market analysis, income approach, and cost approach, to determine the fair market value of the property.

### Potential Returns:

Evaluate the potential returns of the investment, considering factors such as rental income, property appreciation, tax benefits, and cash flow projections. Perform sensitivity analysis to understand the impact of different scenarios on investment returns.

### Real Estate Investment Strategies:

Real estate investment offers a range of strategies to suit different investment goals and risk profiles:

### Buy and Hold Strategy:

Acquire properties with the intention of holding them for the long term, generating rental income, and benefiting from property appreciation over time.

### Fix and Flip Strategy:

Purchase distressed properties at a lower price, renovate or improve them, and sell them quickly for a profit.

**Rental Property Strategy:**

Acquire properties and rent them out to tenants, generating consistent rental income over time.

**Real Estate Investment Trusts (REITs):**

Invest in publicly traded REITs, which allow you to gain exposure to a diversified portfolio of real estate properties and receive dividends from rental income.

**Real Estate Syndication:**

Pool resources with other investors to jointly invest in larger real estate projects, such as apartment complexes or commercial properties, sharing the risks and returns.

**Real Estate Development:**

Engage in real estate development projects, which involve acquiring land or existing properties, obtaining necessary permits, and constructing new properties or renovating existing ones for sale or rental purposes.

**Managing Real Estate Investments:**

Efficient management of real estate investments is crucial for success:

**Property Management:**

Decide whether to manage the property yourself or hire a professional property management company to handle tenant screening, rent collection, property maintenance, and other day-to-day tasks.

**Lease Agreements and Tenant Screening:**

Create thorough lease agreements that outline the terms and conditions of the tenancy. Conduct comprehensive tenant screenings, including credit checks and background checks, to ensure reliable tenants.

**Maintaining and Enhancing Properties:**

Regularly maintain and enhance properties to ensure they remain in good condition and attractive to tenants or potential buyers. This includes addressing repairs, upgrades, and staying up-to-date with market trends.

**Dealing with Tenants and Property Issues:**

Establish good communication and relationships with tenants, promptly address their concerns, and resolve any property-related issues that may arise.

**Risk Management and Insurance:**

Protect your investment by obtaining appropriate insurance coverage, such as property insurance and liability insurance, to mitigate risks associated with property damage, natural disasters, and legal liabilities.

**Tax Considerations in Real Estate Investment:**

Understanding the tax implications of real estate investment is essential:

**Tax Benefits:**

Familiarize yourself with the tax benefits associated with real estate investment, including deductions for mortgage interest, property taxes, depreciation, and expenses related to property management.

**Depreciation and Cost Segregation:**

Understand how to take advantage of depreciation deductions and cost segregation, which allows you to accelerate depreciation on certain components of the property.

**1031 Exchange and Tax Deferral:**

Explore the possibility of utilizing a 1031 exchange, which allows you to defer capital gains taxes by reinvesting the proceeds from the sale of one property into the purchase of another like-kind property.

**Passive Activity Loss Rules:**

Comply with passive activity loss rules, which limit the deduction of losses from rental properties if you have limited participation in managing the property.

**Consultation with Tax Professionals:**

Seek guidance from tax professionals who specialize in real estate investments to ensure compliance with tax laws and optimize tax strategies.

**Real Estate Investment Risks and Challenges:**

Real estate investment involves risks that should be carefully considered:

**Market Volatility and Economic Factors:**

Real estate markets are influenced by various factors, including economic conditions, interest rates, and market cycles. Fluctuations in these factors can impact property values and rental demand.

**Financing Risks and Interest Rates:**

Changes in interest rates can affect the cost of financing, making it crucial to assess the potential impact on cash flow and profitability. Financing risks include the ability to secure loans and refinance properties.

**Property Management Challenges:**

Managing properties and dealing with tenants can present challenges, such as tenant vacancies, maintenance issues, and disputes. Effective property management is essential to mitigate these challenges.

**Regulatory and Legal Risks:**

Real estate investments are subject to various regulations and legal requirements, including zoning laws, building codes, landlord-tenant laws, and property taxes. Non-compliance can result in penalties and legal disputes.

**Real Estate Market Cycles:**

Real estate markets go through cycles of expansion, contraction, and stabilization. Understanding these cycles and their potential impact on property values and rental income is essential for investment success.

**Conclusion:**

Real estate investment offers individuals the opportunity to build wealth, generate passive income, and diversify their investment portfolios. By understanding the key concepts, strategies, considerations, and steps involved in real estate investment, investors can make informed decisions and navigate the market effectively. Thorough market analysis, careful property selection, strategic financing, effective property management, and tax planning are critical for success. Additionally, it is important to continually educate oneself, stay updated on market trends, and adapt strategies to changing market conditions. With diligent research, proper risk management, and a long-term perspective, real estate investment can be a rewarding and profitable venture.

## 7.2    Analysing Property Markets and Trends

Analysing property markets and trends is a crucial step in real estate investment. It involves evaluating various factors that impact property values, rental demand, and investment potential. Understanding market dynamics helps investors make informed decisions and identify profitable investment opportunities. In this guide, we will explore the key aspects of analysing property markets and trends, including market research, data analysis, economic indicators, and emerging trends.

**Market Research:**

Market research forms the foundation of analysing property markets. It involves gathering and analysing data to gain insights into local market conditions and trends. Here are key elements of market research:

**Local Market Area:**

Define the specific market area you are interested in, such as a city, neighbourhood, or region. Focus on areas where you have knowledge or can access reliable information.

**Property Types:**

Identify the types of properties prevalent in the market, such as residential, commercial, or mixed-use.

Understand the supply and demand dynamics for each property type.

**Comparable Sales:**

Analyse recent sales of comparable properties in the area to determine property values. Consider factors such as location, size, condition, and amenities.

**Rental Market Analysis:**

Assess the rental market by examining vacancy rates, rental rates, and rental demand. Evaluate the types of rental properties in demand and the demographics of potential tenants.

**Market Conditions:**

Evaluate the overall market conditions, including factors like inventory levels, average days on market, and buyer/seller dynamics. Determine whether it is a buyer's or seller's market.

**Data Analysis:**

Data analysis plays a critical role in understanding property markets. It involves examining historical and current data to identify trends and patterns. Here are key data analysis techniques:

**Sales Data:**

Analyse sales data to identify price trends, seasonality, and market fluctuations. Look for patterns in property values, sales volumes, and average price per square foot.

**Rental Data:**

Examine rental data, including rental rates, occupancy rates, and rental market trends. Compare rental prices across different property types and locations.

**Market Indicators:**

Evaluate market indicators such as supply and demand ratios, absorption rates, and housing affordability indexes. These indicators provide insights into market stability and the balance between supply and demand.

**Economic Indicators:**

Consider economic indicators like GDP growth, employment rates, and population growth. These indicators impact the overall economy and, subsequently, the real estate market.

**Emerging Data Sources:**

Explore emerging data sources such as online real estate platforms, government databases, and industry reports. These sources provide valuable information on property sales, rental rates, and market trends.

**Economic Indicators:**

Economic indicators provide a broader understanding of the economic health and potential growth of a property market. Consider the following economic indicators:

**GDP Growth:**

Assess the Gross Domestic Product (GDP) growth rate of the region. Higher GDP growth typically indicates a strong economy and potential for real estate market growth.

**Employment Rates:**

Analyse employment rates and job growth in the area. A stable job market and increasing employment rates contribute to housing demand and rental market stability.

**Population Growth:**

Evaluate population growth rates, migration patterns, and demographic trends. Growing populations create demand for housing and can drive property appreciation.

**Interest Rates:**

Monitor interest rate trends set by central banks. Lower interest rates can stimulate borrowing and increase affordability, while higher interest rates may decrease demand.

**Infrastructure and Development:**

Consider planned or ongoing infrastructure projects and developments in the area. These projects can have a significant impact on property values and rental demand.

**Emerging Trends:**

Identifying emerging trends is crucial for staying ahead in the real estate market. Consider the following trends:

**Sustainable and Green Properties:**

Increasing environmental awareness has led to a rising demand for sustainable and energy-efficient properties. Properties with green features and certifications may attract tenants and have long-term value.

**Technology Integration:**

Embrace technological advancements and their impact on the real estate industry. Consider trends like smart homes, virtual tours, and digital marketing strategies to stay competitive.

**Co-Living and Co-Working Spaces:**

The rise of co-living and co-working spaces is transforming the real estate landscape. Assess the demand for these shared spaces and explore investment opportunities.

### Urbanization and Mixed-Use Developments:

Urban areas are experiencing significant growth and revitalization. Mixed-use developments that combine residential, commercial, and retail spaces are gaining popularity.

### Short-Term Rentals and Airbnb:

The rise of short-term rental platforms like Airbnb has disrupted the traditional rental market. Assess the regulatory environment and potential profitability of short-term rentals.

### Market Timing and Investment Strategy:

Understanding property market trends is essential for market timing and developing an investment strategy. Consider the following factors:

### Buyer's Market vs. Seller's Market:

Identify whether it is a buyer's or seller's market. A buyer's market offers more negotiating power, while a seller's market favors sellers.

### Investment Horizon:

Align your investment strategy with your investment horizon. Short-term strategies like fix and flip may require market timing for maximum profitability, while long-term strategies focus on property appreciation and cash flow.

**Risk Assessment:**

Evaluate the risks associated with the property market, including potential economic downturns, interest rate changes, and regulatory risks. Assess the level of risk you are willing to undertake and adjust your strategy accordingly.

**Diversification:**

Consider diversifying your real estate portfolio by investing in different property types or geographic locations. This diversification can help mitigate risks and balance potential returns.

**Conclusion:**

Analyzing property markets and trends is crucial for successful real estate investment. By conducting thorough market research, analyzing data, considering economic indicators, and staying updated on emerging trends, investors can make informed decisions and identify profitable investment opportunities. Market analysis enables investors to understand property values, rental demand, market conditions, and economic factors that influence investment decisions. Additionally, it helps with market timing, strategy development, risk assessment, and portfolio diversification. Continually monitoring property markets and adapting strategies based on market trends and conditions is essential for long-term success in real estate investment.

## 7.3 Strategies for Property Acquisition

Property acquisition is a crucial aspect of real estate investment. The process involves identifying and acquiring properties that align with your investment goals and offer potential for cash flow and appreciation. Implementing effective acquisition strategies is key to finding and securing profitable investment opportunities. In this guide, we will explore various strategies for property acquisition, including traditional methods, off-market opportunities, networking, and leveraging technology.

**Traditional Methods:**

Traditional methods of property acquisition involve utilizing established channels and resources to find investment opportunities. Here are some strategies to consider:

**Real Estate Agents:**

Engage with local real estate agents who specialize in the market area you are interested in. Agents have access to multiple listing services (MLS) and can help you identify properties that meet your criteria.

**Online Listings:**

Explore online platforms and websites that list properties for sale. Popular platforms include Zillow, Realtor.com, and local real estate websites. Regularly review new listings and filter them based on your investment criteria.

**Auctions:**

Attend real estate auctions, which can provide opportunities to acquire properties at a potentially lower price. Auctions may involve foreclosed properties, distressed sales, or properties being sold by motivated sellers.

**For Sale by Owner (FSBO):**

Look for properties being sold directly by the owner. FSBO properties may not be listed on MLS or other platforms, so driving through neighbourhood's or searching local classifieds can help identify these opportunities.

**Off-Market Opportunities:**

Off-market opportunities refer to properties that are not publicly listed for sale. These opportunities can provide advantages, such as less competition and potential for favourable negotiation. Here are some strategies to uncover off-market opportunities:

**Networking:**

Build relationships with local real estate professionals, including wholesalers, property managers, contractors, and other investors. Networking can lead to off-market deals as these professionals often have access to exclusive or pre-market opportunities.

**Direct Mail Marketing:**

Develop a targeted direct mail campaign to reach property owners who may be interested in selling. Send personalized letters or postcards expressing your interest in purchasing their property. This approach can uncover potential off-market opportunities.

**Driving for Dollars:**

Drive through target neighborhoods and look for properties that appear vacant, distressed, or in need of repair. Take note of the property addresses and research the owners to make direct contact and explore potential off-market opportunities.

**Cold Calling:**

Proactively reach out to property owners who may be interested in selling. Cold calling can be an effective way to identify off-market opportunities and initiate direct negotiations.

**Wholesalers:**

Establish relationships with real estate wholesalers who specialize in sourcing off-market deals. Wholesalers often have a network of motivated sellers and can offer discounted properties for quick acquisition.

**Networking and Relationships:**

Building a strong network and cultivating relationships with industry professionals can provide valuable opportunities for property acquisition. Consider the following strategies:

**Real Estate Investment Groups:**

Join local real estate investment groups, clubs, or associations. These groups offer networking events, educational resources, and access to potential investment opportunities through member referrals.

**Industry Events and Conferences:**

Attend real estate conferences, seminars, and workshops. These events bring together industry professionals and provide opportunities for networking, learning, and discovering potential investment opportunities.

**Online Communities and Forums:**

Participate in online real estate communities, such as forums and social media groups. Engage with other investors, share knowledge, and build relationships that can lead to property acquisition opportunities.

**Local Professionals:**

Establish relationships with local professionals, such as attorneys, accountants, lenders, and property managers. These professionals can provide referrals, market insights, and connections to potential investment opportunities.

### Technology and Online Resources:

Leveraging technology and online resources can streamline the property acquisition process and provide access to a broader range of opportunities. Consider the following strategies:

### Property Search Tools:

Utilize online tools and resources to streamline your property search. These tools allow you to filter properties based on specific criteria, such as location, price range, property type, and desired return on investment.

### Real Estate Investment Platforms:

Explore online real estate investment platforms that connect investors with investment opportunities. These platforms may offer access to crowdfunding projects, syndications, or pre-vetted investment deals.

### Data and Analytics:

Use data and analytics tools to analyse market trends, property values, rental rates, and potential investment returns. Access to accurate and up-to-date data can help you make informed decisions during the property acquisition process.

**Property Management Software:**

Implement property management software to streamline property acquisition and management tasks. These tools can help with property analysis, document management, tenant screening, and financial tracking.

**Online Auctions:**

Participate in online real estate auctions, which provide convenience and access to a wider range of properties. Online auctions offer the opportunity to acquire properties from anywhere, without geographic limitations.

**Conclusion:**

Implementing effective strategies for property acquisition is crucial for successful real estate investment. By utilizing traditional methods, exploring off-market opportunities, building a strong network, and leveraging technology, investors can uncover profitable investment opportunities that align with their goals. It is important to remain proactive, conduct thorough due diligence, and stay informed about market trends and emerging opportunities. Remember that each market and investment opportunity is unique, so adapt and tailor your strategies based on local market conditions and your specific investment objectives. With a strategic approach to property acquisition, investors can build a successful real estate portfolio and achieve their financial goals.

## 7.4 Maximizing Returns through Rental Properties and Flipping

Rental properties and flipping are two popular strategies in real estate investment that offer opportunities to maximize returns. Rental properties generate income through rental payments, while flipping involves buying distressed properties, renovating them, and selling them quickly for a profit. This guide explores strategies for maximizing returns through rental properties and flipping, including property selection, financing options, renovation strategies, and market timing considerations.

**Rental Properties:**

Rental properties provide a steady stream of income through rental payments and the potential for long-term appreciation. To maximize returns through rental properties, consider the following strategies:

**Property Selection:**

Choose properties with strong rental potential. Look for properties in desirable locations with amenities, good school districts, proximity to employment centers, and transportation options. Consider the rental demand for different property types, such as single-family homes, multi-family properties, or vacation rentals.

### Cash Flow Analysis:

Conduct a thorough cash flow analysis before purchasing a rental property. Consider expenses such as mortgage payments, property taxes, insurance, maintenance costs, and property management fees. Ensure that the rental income covers these expenses and leaves room for positive cash flow.

### Financing Options:

Explore financing options that optimize returns. Traditional mortgages, private financing, or partnerships can help acquire properties while minimizing upfront costs and maximizing leverage. Consider the interest rates, loan terms, and financing costs associated with different options.

### Property Management:

Effective property management is crucial for maximizing returns on rental properties. Consider whether to manage the property yourself or hire a professional property management company. Property managers handle tasks such as tenant screening, rent collection, property maintenance, and addressing tenant concerns.

### Rental Market Analysis:

Continually analyse the rental market to determine rental rates and adjust them based on market conditions. Stay informed about rental trends, vacancy rates, and rental demand in the area. Regularly review and renew leases to ensure competitive rental rates.

**Tenant Screening:**

Implement a rigorous tenant screening process to minimize tenant turnover and potential issues. Conduct background checks, credit checks, employment verification, and reference checks to ensure reliable and responsible tenants. Quality tenants contribute to steady rental income and reduce the risk of property damage.

**Property Maintenance:**

Maintain the property to attract and retain tenants and protect its value. Respond promptly to repair requests and conduct regular inspections to identify and address maintenance issues. Well-maintained properties are more likely to command higher rental rates and attract quality tenants.

**Rental Rate Optimization:**

Evaluate rental rates periodically to ensure they align with market conditions and maximize returns. Consider factors such as local market trends, property condition, amenities, and tenant demand. Incremental increases in rental rates over time can boost cash flow and returns.

## Flipping:

Flipping involves purchasing distressed properties, renovating them, and selling them quickly for a profit. To maximize returns through flipping, consider the following strategies:

## Property Analysis:

Conduct a thorough analysis of potential flip properties. Look for properties with significant potential for improvement and value appreciation. Consider factors such as location, property condition, market demand, and potential resale value.

## Purchase Price Negotiation:

Negotiate the purchase price to ensure a favourable deal. Assess the property's condition, estimated renovation costs, and potential resale value when determining the maximum purchase price. Aim for a purchase price that allows for a profitable sale after renovation expenses.

## Renovation Budgeting:

Create a detailed budget for renovation expenses. Consider costs for materials, labour, permits, and unforeseen repairs. It's crucial to accurately estimate renovation costs to avoid overspending and eroding potential profits.

### Renovation Strategy:

Develop a renovation strategy that maximizes the property's value while staying within budget. Focus on high-impact improvements that appeal to potential buyers, such as kitchen and bathroom upgrades, flooring, paint, and curb appeal enhancements. Strive for a balance between cost-effective renovations and attractive aesthetics.

### Efficient Project Management:

Efficiently manage the renovation project to minimize costs and time. Ensure proper coordination of contractors, obtain necessary permits, and closely monitor progress. Timely completion of renovations allows for a quicker sale and reduces carrying costs.

### Market Timing:

Consider market conditions and timing when flipping properties. Monitor local market trends, supply and demand dynamics, and property values. Aim to sell the renovated property during a favourable market period when demand is high and prices are favourable.

### Marketing and Sales Strategy:

Develop an effective marketing and sales strategy to attract potential buyers. Utilize professional staging, high-quality listing photos, and targeted marketing efforts to showcase the property's features and appeal.

Work with experienced real estate agents or utilize online platforms to reach a wide audience of potential buyers.

**Cost Control and Profit Margin:**

Carefully control renovation costs to maximize profit margins. Continually assess expenses, identify cost-saving opportunities, and avoid unnecessary or excessive spending. A higher profit margin increases the overall return on investment.

**Conclusion:**

Maximizing returns through rental properties and flipping requires strategic planning, careful analysis, and diligent execution. Rental properties offer steady income streams and long-term appreciation potential, while flipping provides quick profits through renovation and resale. To maximize returns, investors should focus on property selection, financing options, effective property management, market analysis, renovation strategies, and market timing considerations. Thorough due diligence, market research, and ongoing management are essential for success. By implementing these strategies and staying informed about market trends, investors can optimize returns and build a successful real estate portfolio.

# 8. Building a Passive Income Empire

Building a passive income empire involves creating multiple streams of income that generate consistent cash flow with minimal ongoing effort. This empire can provide financial stability, flexibility, and the potential for long-term wealth accumulation. In this guide, we will explore strategies and steps to build a passive income empire, including identifying income sources, creating systems, leveraging technology, and scaling your portfolio.

## 8.1    Creating Multiple Streams of Passive Income

Creating multiple streams of passive income is a powerful wealth-building strategy that can provide financial security and freedom. By diversifying your income sources and generating cash flow with minimal ongoing effort, you can build a robust portfolio that generates income even when you're not actively working. In this guide, we will explore the concept of multiple streams of passive income, the benefits it offers, and strategies to create and manage these income streams effectively.

**Understanding Multiple Streams of Passive Income:**

Multiple streams of passive income refer to having various sources of income that generate cash flow without requiring continuous active involvement. Unlike traditional employment, where you exchange time for money, passive income allows you to earn money while you sleep, travel, or pursue other activities. By diversifying your income sources, you reduce reliance on a single income stream, increase your overall income potential, and build resilience against financial uncertainty.

**Benefits of Multiple Streams of Passive Income:**

Creating multiple streams of passive income offers several benefits.

**Financial Security:**

Relying on a single income source puts you at risk of financial instability. By diversifying your income streams, you create a safety net that can sustain you even if one source of income is disrupted or underperforms.

**Income Stability:**

Passive income streams can provide a steady cash flow, regardless of fluctuations in the job market or economic conditions. This stability allows you to maintain your lifestyle and meet financial obligations consistently.

**Flexibility and Freedom:**

Multiple streams of passive income provide flexibility and freedom to choose how you spend your time.

You're not tied to a traditional job, and you have more control over your schedule and pursuits.

**Wealth Accumulation:**

Passive income streams can accelerate wealth accumulation by allowing you to reinvest the excess cash flow into new income-generating assets or investments. Over time, this can lead to compounding returns and exponential wealth growth.

**Reducing Dependency on Active Work:**

By creating passive income streams, you reduce your dependency on actively trading time for money. This gives you the opportunity to pursue other passions, spend time with loved ones, or explore new ventures.

**Strategies to Create Multiple Streams of Passive Income:**

**Rental Properties:**

Investing in real estate and generating rental income is a popular and proven strategy for creating passive income. Consider the following steps:

**Research and Analysis:**

Study the real estate market to identify areas with high rental demand and potential for property appreciation. Analyse rental rates, vacancy rates, and property prices to determine the profitability of potential investments.

**Property Acquisition:**

Purchase residential or commercial properties that align with your investment goals and budget. Conduct thorough due diligence, including property inspections, financial analysis, and market research.

**Property Management:**

Decide whether to manage the properties yourself or hire a property management company. Property managers handle tasks such as tenant screening, rent collection, maintenance, and property marketing.

**Cash Flow Optimization:**

Aim for positive cash flow by ensuring that rental income covers mortgage payments, property expenses, and leaves room for profit. Regularly review rental rates and adjust them based on market conditions.

**Long-Term Appreciation:**

Real estate properties have the potential to appreciate in value over time. Monitor market trends and consider strategies to maximize property value, such as renovations or adding amenities.

**Dividend-Paying Stocks:**

Investing in dividend-paying stocks can provide a passive income stream through regular dividend payments. Consider the following steps:

**Research and Analysis:**

Identify stable companies with a history of consistent dividend payments. Evaluate factors such as the company's financial health, dividend yield, dividend growth rate, and industry trends.

**Portfolio Diversification:**

Build a diversified portfolio of dividend-paying stocks across different sectors and industries. This reduces the risk of relying on a single company or sector.

**Dividend Reinvestment:**

Consider reinvesting dividends to compound your returns over time. Dividend reinvestment plans (DRIPs) allow you to automatically reinvest dividends in additional shares of the stock.

**Regular Monitoring:**

Stay informed about company performance, financial news, and dividend announcements. Monitor dividend growth rates and make adjustments to your portfolio as needed.

**Peer-to-Peer Lending:**

Participating in peer-to-peer lending platforms allows you to lend money to individuals or businesses in exchange for interest payments. Consider the following steps:

**Platform Research:**

Evaluate peer-to-peer lending platforms to find reputable ones that align with your risk tolerance and investment goals. Consider factors such as loan types, borrower vetting processes, historical loan performance, and platform fees.

**Risk Assessment:**

Assess the creditworthiness of borrowers by reviewing their credit profiles, income stability, and loan purpose. Choose loans with lower default rates and consider diversifying your investments across multiple loans.

**Investment Allocation:**

Determine the amount of capital you're willing to invest and allocate it across different loans to spread the risk. Some platforms offer automated investment tools that diversify your portfolio across multiple loans.

**Loan Monitoring and Reinvestment:**

Regularly monitor your loans, including interest payments and potential defaults. Reinvest the repaid principal and interest into new loans to maintain a consistent cash flow.

## Online Business and Digital Products:

Building an online business and creating digital products can generate passive income through sales and royalties. Consider the following steps:

### Identify a Niche:

Determine a target audience or market segment that aligns with your skills, expertise, or interests. Research the market to identify gaps or opportunities.

### Product Creation:

Develop digital products such as e-books, online courses, software, or membership sites that provide value to your target audience. Invest time upfront to create high-quality products that can generate income over an extended period.

### Marketing and Sales:

Implement effective marketing strategies to reach your target audience and promote your products. Utilize content marketing, social media, email marketing, and search engine optimization to drive traffic and sales.

**Automation and Scalability:**

Utilize technology and automation tools to streamline your business operations. This includes sales funnels, payment processing systems, customer support automation, and email autoresponders.

**Continuous Improvement:**

Regularly update and improve your digital products to meet the evolving needs of your audience. Gather feedback, monitor customer satisfaction, and implement enhancements to increase sales and customer retention.

**Royalties and Licensing:**

Generating passive income through royalties and licensing involves creating intellectual property or licensing existing assets to others. Consider the following steps:

**Intellectual Property Creation:**

Create original content such as books, music, artwork, or software that has the potential to generate ongoing royalties. Protect your intellectual property rights through copyrights, patents, or trademarks.

**Licensing Agreements:**

Explore opportunities to license your intellectual property to others for a fee. This can include licensing your content to publishers, music platforms, software companies, or manufacturers.

**Royalty Agreements:**

Enter into royalty agreements with distributors, retailers, or platforms that distribute your products. This allows you to earn ongoing income based on sales or usage of your intellectual property.

**Legal Considerations:**

Seek legal advice to ensure proper protection of your intellectual property rights and to negotiate favourable licensing or royalty agreements.

**Continuous Promotion:**

Market your intellectual property to maximize exposure and increase the potential for continuous royalties or licensing income. Utilize marketing strategies, partnerships, and online platforms to reach a wider audience.

**Affiliate Marketing:**

Affiliate marketing involves promoting other people's products or services and earning a commission for each sale or referral. Consider the following steps:

**Niche Selection:**

Choose a niche or industry that aligns with your interests and target audience. Research affiliate programs and products that are relevant to your niche.

### Content Creation:

Create high-quality content such as blog posts, videos, or social media posts that provide value and promote affiliate products. Focus on building trust with your audience and recommending products that genuinely meet their needs.

### Affiliate Program Selection:

Join reputable affiliate programs or networks that offer products or services related to your niche. Consider factors such as commission rates, cookie durations, and payment terms.

### Promotion and Conversion Optimization:

Implement marketing strategies to promote affiliate products effectively. Utilize SEO, social media marketing, email marketing, and conversion optimization techniques to drive traffic and increase conversions.

### Performance Tracking:

Monitor your affiliate marketing performance using tracking tools and analytics. Identify which products, promotions, or channels generate the most sales and optimize your strategies accordingly.

### Rental Income from Assets:

Apart from real estate, you can generate rental income from other assets, such as vehicles, equipment, or storage spaces. Consider the following steps:

### Asset Selection:

Determine which assets you can rent out to generate income. This can include cars, motorcycles, boats, RVs, construction equipment, or storage units.

### Rental Market Research:

Analyse the demand and rental rates for your chosen assets in your target market. Consider factors such as location, seasonality, competition, and local regulations.

### Rental Agreements and Contracts:

Develop rental agreements or contracts that outline the terms and conditions of renting your assets. Include details such as rental rates, security deposits, insurance requirements, and maintenance responsibilities.

### Marketing and Promotion:

Advertise your rental assets through online platforms, local classifieds, or targeted marketing channels. Highlight the features, benefits, and competitive pricing of your rentals to attract potential customers.

**Maintenance and Customer Support:**

Maintain your assets in good condition and provide excellent customer support to renters. Promptly address any maintenance issues or concerns to ensure customer satisfaction and repeat business.

**Systematize and Automate:**

To manage multiple streams of passive income effectively, it's essential to systematize and automate your processes. Consider the following strategies:

**Standard Operating Procedures:**

Develop standard operating procedures (SOPs) for each income stream. Document the steps, workflows, and best practices involved in managing and growing each income source.

**Outsourcing and Delegation:**

Identify tasks that can be outsourced or delegated to others. This can include property management, content creation, customer support, bookkeeping, or administrative tasks. Hiring virtual assistants or contractors can help free up your time and focus on strategic activities.

**Technology and Automation Tools:**

Utilize technology and automation tools to streamline your operations. This includes project management software, customer relationship management (CRM) systems, email autoresponders, and financial management platforms.

### Continuous Monitoring and Optimization:

Regularly review the performance of each income stream and make data-driven decisions to optimize your results. Monitor key metrics, analyse trends, and identify areas for improvement.

### Scaling Your Passive Income Empire:

Once you have established and optimized your initial passive income streams, you can scale your empire by expanding your existing streams or diversifying into new income sources. Consider the following strategies:

### Portfolio Expansion:

Acquire additional rental properties, invest in new dividend-paying stocks, or expand your peer-to-peer lending portfolio. Continuously monitor market conditions and identify opportunities for growth.

### Product Line Extension:

Develop new digital products, courses, or software to cater to different segments of your target audience.

Leverage your existing customer base and marketing channels to promote new offerings.

**Strategic Partnerships:**

Collaborate with other entrepreneurs or businesses to create joint ventures or partnerships. Pool your resources, expertise, and networks to create new income-generating opportunities.

**Acquisitions or Investments:**

Explore opportunities to acquire or invest in existing businesses, real estate projects, or income-generating assets. This allows you to leverage the expertise of others and benefit from established income streams.

**Conclusion:**

Creating multiple streams of passive income is a powerful wealth-building strategy that offers financial security, flexibility, and the potential for long-term wealth accumulation. By diversifying your income sources and leveraging various strategies such as rental properties, dividend-paying stocks, online businesses, royalties, and affiliate marketing, you can build a robust portfolio that generates income even when you're not actively working. Remember to conduct thorough research, continuously optimize your income streams, and systematize your processes to effectively manage and scale your passive income empire. With dedication, strategic planning, and persistence, you can create a sustainable and profitable portfolio of passive income streams that brings you closer to financial independence and freedom.

## 8.2  Managing and Expanding Existing Ventures

Managing and expanding existing ventures is a critical aspect of business growth and long-term success. As businesses evolve, it becomes essential to effectively manage operations, adapt to changing market dynamics, and explore new opportunities for expansion. In this guide, we will explore strategies and best practices for managing and expanding existing ventures, including organizational management, operational efficiency, customer retention, innovation, and strategic planning.

**Organizational Management:**

Effective organizational management is crucial for managing and expanding existing ventures. Consider the following strategies:

**Clear Vision and Mission:**

Ensure that the venture's vision and mission are well-defined and communicated to all stakeholders. This provides a clear sense of purpose and direction for the organization.

**Leadership Development:**

Invest in leadership development programs to empower and develop employees at all levels. Foster a culture of continuous learning and growth to enhance leadership capabilities within the organization.

**Talent Acquisition and Retention:**

Attract and retain top talent by implementing effective recruitment and retention strategies. Create a positive work environment, offer competitive compensation packages, and provide opportunities for career advancement.

**Effective Communication:**

Establish open and transparent communication channels within the organization. Foster a culture of collaboration, feedback, and idea-sharing to enhance teamwork and overall productivity.

**Performance Management:**

Implement performance management systems to set clear goals, provide regular feedback, and recognize achievements. Establish Key Performance Indicators (KPIs) to measure individual and team performance.

**Operational Efficiency:**

Efficient operations are essential for managing and expanding existing ventures. Consider the following strategies:

**Process Optimization:**

Continually review and optimize business processes to enhance efficiency. Identify bottlenecks, eliminate redundant tasks, and streamline workflows to improve productivity and reduce costs.

**Technology Adoption:**

Embrace technology solutions to automate and streamline operations. Implement systems for inventory management, customer relationship management (CRM), accounting, and other core functions to improve efficiency and accuracy.

**Supply Chain Management:**

Develop strong relationships with suppliers and optimize the supply chain. Streamline procurement processes, negotiate favourable terms, and monitor supplier performance to ensure timely delivery of goods and services.

**Quality Control:**

Implement rigorous quality control measures to ensure consistent product or service delivery. Monitor quality standards, conduct regular inspections, and gather customer feedback to drive continuous improvement.

**Cost Management:**

Continuously evaluate costs and identify areas for cost reduction. Implement cost-saving measures such as energy efficiency, waste reduction, and supplier negotiation to optimize profitability.

**Customer Retention and Satisfaction:**

Customer retention and satisfaction are key to managing and expanding existing ventures. Consider the following strategies:

**Customer Relationship Management (CRM):**

Implement a CRM system to effectively manage customer interactions and relationships. Track customer preferences, purchase history, and feedback to personalize marketing efforts and improve customer experience.

**Customer Service Excellence:**

Provide exceptional customer service by promptly addressing customer inquiries, complaints, and requests. Train employees on effective customer service techniques and empower them to resolve issues.

**Loyalty Programs:**

Develop loyalty programs to reward and retain loyal customers. Offer incentives, discounts, or exclusive benefits to encourage repeat purchases and foster long-term customer relationships.

**Feedback and Surveys:**

Regularly gather customer feedback through surveys, focus groups, or online reviews. Use customer insights to identify areas for improvement and make data-driven decisions to enhance the customer experience.

**Personalized Marketing:**

Leverage customer data to personalize marketing efforts. Segment customers based on preferences, demographics, or purchase behaviour to deliver targeted marketing messages that resonate with their needs and preferences.

**Innovation and Adaptability:**

Innovation and adaptability are crucial for managing and expanding existing ventures in a rapidly changing business landscape. Consider the following strategies:

**Market Research and Analysis:**

Continuously monitor market trends, customer preferences, and competitive landscape. Conduct market research to identify emerging opportunities and stay ahead of industry trends.

**Product and Service Innovation:**

Regularly assess and enhance existing products or services to meet evolving customer needs. Foster a culture of innovation and encourage employees to contribute ideas for product or service enhancements.

**New Market Exploration:**

Explore new markets or customer segments to expand your venture's reach. Identify untapped opportunities, conduct market entry analysis, and develop tailored strategies to enter new markets successfully.

**Partnerships and Alliances:**

Form strategic partnerships or alliances to leverage complementary resources and capabilities. Collaborate with other businesses or industry experts to access new markets, share expertise, and accelerate growth.

**Continuous Learning:**

Encourage a learning culture within the organization. Invest in employee training and development programs to enhance skills, knowledge, and adaptability to technological advancements or industry changes.

**Strategic Planning:**

Strategic planning is essential for managing and expanding existing ventures effectively. Consider the following strategies:

**Goal Setting:**

Set clear, measurable, and time-bound goals for your venture. Align goals with your vision and mission, and regularly review progress towards achieving them.

**SWOT Analysis:**

Conduct a comprehensive analysis of your venture's strengths, weaknesses, opportunities, and threats (SWOT analysis). This analysis helps identify areas for improvement and opportunities for growth.

**Competitive Analysis:**

Assess your venture's competitive landscape and identify your unique value proposition. Understand competitors' strengths and weaknesses to differentiate your offering effectively.

**Long-Term Planning:**

Develop a long-term strategic plan that outlines your venture's growth objectives, target markets, competitive positioning, and resource allocation. Regularly review and update the strategic plan to reflect changing market conditions.

**Risk Management:**

Identify and manage potential risks and uncertainties that may impact your venture's growth. Develop contingency plans and risk mitigation strategies to minimize potential disruptions.

**Conclusion:**

Effectively managing and expanding existing ventures requires a combination of strategic thinking, operational excellence, customer focus, and adaptability. By implementing strategies for organizational management, operational efficiency, customer retention, innovation, and strategic planning, businesses can navigate the challenges of growth and seize new opportunities. Continually monitor market trends, engage employees, and foster a culture of innovation to stay ahead in a competitive business landscape. With a strong foundation and effective management practices, existing ventures can thrive, expand their reach, and achieve long-term success.

## 8.3　Leveraging Other People's Resources and Expertise

In business, success often depends on utilizing available resources and expertise effectively. However, it is not always necessary to possess all the resources or expertise within your own organization. By leveraging other people's resources and expertise, you can tap into a broader network, access specialized knowledge, and benefit from shared resources. In this guide, we will explore strategies for leveraging other people's resources and expertise to enhance your business operations, expand your capabilities, and drive growth.

**Networking and Partnerships:**

Networking and forming strategic partnerships are effective ways to leverage other people's resources and expertise. Consider the following strategies:

**Industry Associations and Events:**

Join industry associations and attend relevant conferences, trade shows, and networking events. Engage with professionals in your field, exchange knowledge, and explore potential collaborations.

**Collaborative Partnerships:**

Identify businesses or individuals that complement your offerings or have similar target audiences. Form collaborative partnerships to leverage each other's resources, share marketing efforts, and expand your reach.

**Supplier and Vendor Relationships:**

Cultivate strong relationships with reliable suppliers and vendors. They can provide access to resources, negotiate favourable terms, and offer valuable industry insights.

**Mentors and Advisors:**

Seek guidance from experienced mentors or industry experts who can share their knowledge and offer advice on business strategies, operations, and growth opportunities.

**Outsourcing and Freelancers:**

Outsourcing certain tasks or hiring freelancers allows you to leverage specialized expertise without incurring the costs of full-time employees. Consider the following strategies:

**Task Evaluation:**

Assess your organization's core competencies and identify non-core activities that can be outsourced. This may include functions such as IT support, accounting, marketing, or graphic design.

**Freelancers and Contractors:**

Hire freelancers or contractors to handle specific projects or tasks. Platforms like Upwork and Freelancer provide access to a wide range of skilled professionals who can contribute their expertise on a project basis.

**Offshore Outsourcing:**

Consider outsourcing certain tasks or processes to offshore service providers. This can help reduce costs while leveraging specialized expertise in areas like customer support, software development, or data entry.

**Virtual Assistants:**

Engage virtual assistants to handle administrative tasks, appointment scheduling, email management, or research. They can provide support remotely, freeing up your time to focus on core business activities.

**Collaborative Spaces and Co-working:**

Collaborative spaces and co-working environments provide opportunities to interact with professionals from diverse backgrounds, industries, and skill sets. Consider the following strategies:

**Co-working Spaces:**

Join co-working spaces that bring together professionals from various fields. These spaces foster collaboration, networking, and the sharing of resources and expertise.

### Industry Hubs and Incubators:

Explore industry-specific hubs or incubators that offer shared resources, mentorship programs, and networking opportunities. These environments facilitate collaboration and access to specialized expertise.

### Knowledge Sharing Platforms:

Participate in online communities, forums, or knowledge-sharing platforms where professionals share their expertise and experiences. Engage in discussions, seek advice, and contribute your own knowledge to leverage the collective wisdom of the community.

### Joint Ventures and Alliances:

Joint ventures and alliances allow businesses to pool their resources, capabilities, and expertise to pursue common objectives. Consider the following strategies:

### Strategic Alliances:

Form alliances with businesses that have complementary offerings or target markets. This allows you to combine resources, share marketing efforts, and expand your customer base.

**Joint Ventures:**

Explore opportunities to establish joint ventures with other businesses to pursue specific projects, enter new markets, or develop new products or services. This enables you to leverage each other's resources, expertise, and market presence.

**Resource Sharing:**

Collaborate with other businesses to share physical resources, such as equipment, warehouses, or distribution channels. This can reduce costs, improve operational efficiency, and enhance your value proposition.

**Crowdsourcing and Open Innovation:**

Crowdsourcing and open innovation involve harnessing the collective intelligence and expertise of a diverse group of individuals to solve problems or generate ideas. Consider the following strategies:

**Idea Contests and Challenges:**

Launch idea contests or challenges to solicit innovative ideas from external contributors. Offer rewards or recognition for the best ideas and leverage the creativity and expertise of a broader audience.

### Crowdfunding:

Utilize crowdfunding platforms to raise funds for specific projects or initiatives. This allows you to leverage the financial resources and support of a community of backers who share an interest in your venture.

### User-generated Content:

Encourage customers or users to contribute content, testimonials, or reviews that can enhance your marketing efforts. Leverage their expertise and experiences to build trust and credibility with your target audience.

### Knowledge Sharing and Training:

Leveraging other people's expertise also involves fostering a culture of knowledge sharing and continuous learning within your organization. Consider the following strategies:

### Internal Knowledge Sharing:

Establish internal platforms or processes that facilitate the sharing of knowledge, best practices, and lessons learned. Encourage employees to document and share their expertise with their colleagues.

### Cross-functional Training:

Provide opportunities for employees to learn from colleagues in different departments or disciplines. This promotes cross-functional collaboration and the sharing of diverse perspectives and expertise.

**External Training and Development:**

Invest in training programs, workshops, or conferences to enhance the skills and knowledge of your employees. This allows them to stay updated with industry trends and leverage external expertise.

**Industry Experts and Consultants:**

Engage industry experts or consultants for specialized training sessions or workshops. Their expertise can provide valuable insights and help your organization develop new capabilities.

**Conclusion:**

Leveraging other people's resources and expertise is a powerful strategy for enhancing your business operations, expanding your capabilities, and driving growth. By networking, for ming strategic partnerships, outsourcing tasks, utilizing co-working spaces, exploring joint ventures, leveraging crowdsourcing, and promoting knowledge sharing, businesses can tap into a broader network, access specialized knowledge, and benefit from shared resources. It is important to approach these collaborations with clear objectives, effective communication, and a win-win mindset. With effective utilization of other people's resources and expertise, businesses can unlock new opportunities, drive innovation, and achieve long-term success in a rapidly evolving business landscape.

## 8.4     Innovating and Adapting to Market Changes

In today's fast-paced and ever-evolving business landscape, the ability to innovate and adapt to market changes is crucial for the long-term success of any organization. Market dynamics, customer preferences, and technological advancements are constantly evolving, creating both opportunities and challenges for businesses. To stay competitive and relevant, organizations must foster a culture of innovation, continuously monitor market trends, and adapt their strategies, products, and services accordingly. In this guide, we will explore strategies and best practices for innovating and adapting to market changes effectively.

**Embracing a Culture of Innovation:**

Innovation starts with cultivating a culture that encourages and rewards creativity, experimentation, and continuous improvement. Consider the following strategies:

**Leadership Support:**

Leaders should set the tone by championing innovation and providing the necessary resources and support. Foster an environment where employees feel empowered to contribute their ideas and take calculated risks.

### Cross-functional Collaboration:

Encourage collaboration and the exchange of ideas across different departments and teams. Break down silos and create opportunities for interdisciplinary collaboration to foster creativity and generate innovative solutions.

### Idea Generation Platforms:

Implement platforms or processes that facilitate the generation and evaluation of ideas. This can include suggestion boxes, innovation challenges, or dedicated innovation teams that are responsible for identifying and developing new ideas.

### Recognition and Rewards:

Recognize and reward employees who contribute innovative ideas or successfully implement innovative initiatives. This reinforces the importance of innovation within the organization and motivates others to actively participate.

### Monitoring Market Trends:

To adapt to market changes, it is essential to stay informed about the latest trends, customer preferences, and emerging technologies. Consider the following strategies:

**Market Research:**

Conduct regular market research to gather insights into customer needs, preferences, and behaviours. This can involve surveys, focus groups, customer interviews, and data analysis to identify emerging trends and shifting market dynamics.

Competitive Analysis:

Monitor competitors and their strategies to identify emerging threats and opportunities. Analyse their product offerings, marketing tactics, pricing strategies, and customer feedback to gain a competitive advantage.

**Technology Monitoring:**

Keep a pulse on technological advancements relevant to your industry. Stay informed about new technologies, tools, or platforms that can enhance your products, services, or operational efficiency.

**Customer Feedback and Reviews:**

Actively seek feedback from customers through surveys, reviews, and social media monitoring. Pay attention to their comments, suggestions, and pain points to identify areas for improvement and innovation.

### Agile Decision-Making:

To adapt quickly to market changes, organizations need to embrace agile decision-making processes. Consider the following strategies:

### Data-Driven Decision-Making:

Utilize data and analytics to inform decision-making processes. Collect and analyse relevant data to understand customer behaviour, market trends, and the impact of potential changes or innovations.

### Rapid Prototyping and Testing:

Adopt an iterative approach to product development and innovation. Create prototypes or minimum viable products (MVPs) and gather feedback from customers to validate assumptions, make improvements, and accelerate the innovation process.

### Cross-Functional Decision-Making:

Involve key stakeholders from different functions or departments in decision-making processes. This ensures diverse perspectives and expertise are considered, leading to well-rounded and informed decisions.

### Fail Fast, Learn Fast:

Encourage a culture where failures are viewed as learning opportunities. Embrace the concept of failing fast and learning from mistakes to iterate and improve.

**Product and Service Innovation:**

Innovation in products and services is vital for staying relevant in the market. Consider the following strategies:

**Customer-Centric Approach:**

Place the customer at the center of the innovation process. Understand their needs, pain points, and aspirations to develop products and services that address their specific challenges or desires.

**Continuous Improvement:**

Adopt a mindset of continuous improvement for existing products and services. Regularly assess customer feedback, conduct usability testing, and gather insights to identify areas for enhancement or refinement.

**New Product Development:**

Encourage cross-functional collaboration to generate ideas for new products or services. Implement robust product development processes, including market validation, prototyping, testing, and commercialization.

**Incremental and Disruptive Innovation:**

Balance incremental innovation (enhancing existing products) with disruptive innovation (introducing entirely new concepts). Disruptive innovations can drive significant market shifts and create new opportunities for growth.

**Customer-Centric Marketing and Sales:**

Adapting marketing and sales strategies to evolving market dynamics is crucial. Consider the following strategies:

**Persona Development:**

Develop detailed customer personas to understand target customers' needs, motivations, and preferences. Tailor marketing messages, channels, and campaigns to resonate with specific customer segments.

**Digital Marketing and Social Media:**

Embrace digital marketing and leverage social media platforms to reach and engage with customers. Monitor social media conversations, track engagement metrics, and use data analytics to optimize marketing efforts.

**Agile Campaigns:**

Implement agile marketing campaigns that can quickly adapt to market changes. Continuously monitor campaign performance, gather customer feedback, and make real-time adjustments to improve effectiveness.

**Sales Enablement:**

Provide sales teams with the tools, resources, and training needed to adapt to changing customer demands. Equip them with up-to-date market insights, competitive intelligence, and effective sales techniques.

### Continuous Learning and Adaptation:

To adapt successfully to market changes, organizations must foster a culture of continuous learning and adaptation. Consider the following strategies:

### Training and Development:

Invest in employee training programs to develop new skills and enhance knowledge. This can include workshops, seminars, online courses, or external certifications to keep employees updated with industry trends and emerging technologies.

### Continuous Improvement Processes:

Implement continuous improvement processes, such as Lean or Six Sigma methodologies, to identify inefficiencies, eliminate waste, and optimize operational processes.

### Agile Project Management:

Embrace agile project management methodologies, such as Scrum or Kanban, to facilitate adaptive planning, collaboration, and iterative delivery of projects. This enables flexibility and responsiveness to changing market conditions.

**Regular Evaluation and Feedback:**

Establish mechanisms for regularly evaluating performance, gathering feedback, and soliciting suggestions from employees. Use this feedback to identify areas for improvement, refine strategies, and adapt to market changes.

**Conclusion:**

Innovating and adapting to market changes is essential for organizations to stay competitive, drive growth, and meet the evolving needs of customers. By fostering a culture of innovation, monitoring market trends, embracing agile decision-making, investing in product and service innovation, adopting customer-centric marketing and sales strategies, and promoting continuous learning and adaptation, businesses can navigate market changes successfully. The key is to remain agile, responsive, and customer-focused, continually scanning the market for opportunities, and proactively adjusting strategies to thrive in an ever-changing business landscape.

# 9. Wealth Preservation and Growth

Preserving and growing wealth is a fundamental goal for individuals and businesses alike. Whether you have accumulated wealth through investments, business ventures, or inheritance, it is essential to adopt strategies that protect your assets and generate sustainable growth over time. In this guide, we will explore key principles and strategies for wealth preservation and growth, including risk management, diversification, asset allocation, tax planning, and long-term investment strategies.

## 9.1     Estate Planning and Asset Protection

Estate planning and asset protection are essential components of comprehensive wealth management. Proper estate planning ensures the orderly distribution of assets upon death and minimizes the tax burden on beneficiaries. Asset protection strategies aim to shield assets from potential risks, such as lawsuits, creditors, or financial crises. In this guide, we will explore the importance of estate planning and asset protection, key elements of an estate plan, and strategies to protect your assets.

**Importance of Estate Planning:**

Estate planning involves creating a plan for the management and distribution of your assets during your lifetime and after your death. It helps protect your family, preserve wealth, and ensure that your wishes are carried out. Consider the following reasons why estate planning is crucial:

**Wealth Distribution:**

Estate planning allows you to determine how your assets will be distributed among your beneficiaries, minimizing disputes and potential conflicts.

**Minimizing Taxes:**

Proper estate planning can help minimize estate taxes, gift taxes, and income taxes, ensuring that more of your wealth is preserved for your loved ones.

**Guardianship for Minor Children:**

Estate planning allows you to nominate guardians for minor children, ensuring they are cared for by individuals you trust.

**Incapacity Planning:**

Estate planning includes documents such as a durable power of attorney and healthcare proxy, which designate trusted individuals to make financial and medical decisions on your behalf if you become incapacitated.

**Charitable Giving:**

Estate planning provides an opportunity to support charitable causes and leave a legacy through philanthropic giving.

**Elements of an Estate Plan:**

A comprehensive estate plan typically includes several key elements. Consider the following components:

**Will:**

A will is a legal document that outlines how your assets will be distributed upon your death. It allows you to name beneficiaries, appoint an executor to carry out your wishes, and designate guardians for minor children.

**Trusts:**

Trusts are legal entities that hold and manage assets for the benefit of beneficiaries. They can provide various benefits, such as avoiding probate, minimizing taxes, protecting assets, and ensuring ongoing management of assets for minor children or individuals with special needs.

**Beneficiary Designations:**

Review and update beneficiary designations on life insurance policies, retirement accounts, and other financial accounts to ensure they align with your estate planning goals.

### Healthcare Directives:

Documents such as a living will and healthcare proxy allow you to express your medical treatment preferences and designate someone to make healthcare decisions on your behalf if you are unable to do so.

### Power of Attorney:

A power of attorney grants someone the authority to handle financial and legal matters on your behalf. This ensures that your affairs are managed in the event of incapacity or when you are unable to make decisions yourself.

### Letter of Instruction:

Although not legally binding, a letter of instruction provides guidance to your loved ones regarding funeral arrangements, preferences for end-of-life care, and the location of important documents.

### Strategies for Asset Protection:

Asset protection involves safeguarding your wealth from potential risks and legal claims. Consider the following strategies:

### Business Structures:

If you own a business, consider using legal entities such as corporations or limited liability companies (LLCs) to separate your personal assets from business liabilities. This can help protect your personal assets in case of lawsuits or debts related to the business.

**Trusts:**

Certain trusts, such as irrevocable trusts, can provide a level of asset protection. Assets placed in an irrevocable trust are no longer considered part of your personal estate and may be shielded from creditors.

**Homestead Exemption:**

In some jurisdictions, a homestead exemption protects the equity in your primary residence from creditors. Understanding the homestead exemption laws in your state can help protect your home from potential claims.

**Insurance Coverage:**

Maintain adequate insurance coverage to protect against potential risks. This includes homeowner's insurance, automobile insurance, liability insurance, and umbrella policies that provide additional coverage beyond the limits of primary policies.

**Retirement Accounts:**

Assets held in qualified retirement accounts, such as 401(k)s or IRAs, are generally protected from creditors under federal bankruptcy laws. Contributing to retirement accounts can be a strategy for asset protection.

**Family Limited Partnerships (FLPs):**

FLPs can be used to transfer assets to family members while maintaining control and protecting assets from potential creditors. However, FLPs require careful planning and adherence to legal requirements.

**Offshore Asset Protection Trusts:**

Some individuals choose to establish offshore trusts in jurisdictions with favourable asset protection laws. These trusts can provide an additional layer of protection but require careful consideration and expert guidance due to legal complexities and potential tax implications.

**Regular Review and Updates:**

Estate plans and asset protection strategies should be reviewed periodically to ensure they align with your evolving circumstances and legal changes. Consider the following practices:

**Regular Review:**

Review your estate plan and asset protection strategies at least once every few years or whenever significant life events occur, such as marriage, divorce, birth of children, or substantial changes in financial circumstances.

**Professional Guidance:**

Consult with an experienced estate planning attorney or financial advisor to ensure that your estate plan is up to date and reflects your current wishes and objectives.

**Beneficiary Designations:**

Regularly review beneficiary designations on financial accounts, insurance policies, and retirement plans to ensure they reflect your intentions and account for any changes in family circumstances.

**Document Storage and Accessibility:**

Maintain an organized system for storing and accessing your estate planning documents. Inform trusted individuals, such as family members or your attorney, about the location of your estate planning documents and how to access them when needed.

**Conclusion:**

Estate planning and asset protection are crucial elements of comprehensive wealth management. By creating a well-structured estate plan, you can ensure that your assets are distributed according to your wishes, minimize tax liabilities, protect your loved ones, and maintain control over your financial affairs. Implementing effective asset protection strategies can safeguard your wealth from potential risks and legal claims. Regularly reviewing and updating your estate plan, seeking professional guidance, and staying informed about changes in laws or regulations will help ensure the continued effectiveness of your estate plan and asset protection strategies.

## 9.2    Tax Optimization Strategies

Tax optimization is a key aspect of financial planning, both for individuals and businesses. By implementing effective tax strategies, you can legally minimize your tax liability, maximize your after-tax income, and optimize your overall financial position. In this guide, we will explore various tax optimization strategies that can help individuals and businesses reduce their tax burden, take advantage of available tax incentives, and make the most of their financial resources.

**Understanding the Tax Landscape:**

To effectively optimize your taxes, it is important to have a solid understanding of the tax landscape. Consider the following aspects:

**Tax Rates and Brackets:**

Familiarize yourself with the applicable tax rates and brackets for different types of income, such as ordinary income, capital gains, and dividends. This will help you assess the impact of different strategies on your overall tax liability.

**Deductions and Credits:**

Learn about available deductions and tax credits that you may qualify for. Deductions reduce your taxable income, while tax credits directly reduce your tax liability.

**Tax Law Changes:**

Stay informed about changes in tax laws and regulations. Changes in tax legislation can impact your tax planning strategies and may create new opportunities for tax optimization.

**Effective Income Tax Planning for Individuals:**

Income tax planning strategies can help individuals reduce their taxable income and minimize their tax liability. Consider the following strategies:

**Retirement Contributions:**

Contribute to tax-advantaged retirement accounts such as 401(k)s, IRAs, or SEP IRAs. Contributions to these accounts are typically tax-deductible, and the investment growth is tax-deferred until withdrawal.

**Health Savings Accounts (HSAs):**

Contribute to an HSA if you have a high-deductible health insurance plan. HSA contributions are tax-deductible, and withdrawals used for qualified medical expenses are tax-free.

**Itemized Deductions:**

Evaluate whether itemizing deductions or taking the standard deduction is more advantageous for your situation. Itemized deductions can include mortgage interest, property taxes, state and local taxes, and charitable contributions.

**Tax-Loss Harvesting:**

Offset capital gains by selling investments that have declined in value. The capital losses can be used to offset capital gains and potentially reduce your tax liability.

**Timing of Income and Expenses:**

Consider the timing of income and expenses to optimize your tax liability. For example, if you expect higher income in the current year, you may want to defer certain income to the following year or accelerate deductible expenses into the current year.

**Tax-Efficient Investments:**

Consider investing in tax-efficient investment vehicles such as index funds or exchange-traded funds (ETFs) that generate minimal taxable distributions. This can help minimize your tax liability on investment income.

**Business Tax Optimization Strategies:**

Businesses can implement various strategies to optimize their tax position. Consider the following approaches:

**Entity Structure:**

Choose the most advantageous legal entity structure for your business. Sole proprietorships, partnerships, S corporations, and C corporations have different tax implications. Consult with a tax advisor to determine the most tax-efficient structure for your specific circumstances.

**Expense Deductions:**

Take advantage of available business expense deductions. Keep detailed records and document all legitimate business expenses to maximize your deductions. This can include costs related to office space, equipment, travel, professional services, and employee benefits.

**Employee Benefits:**

Offer tax-efficient employee benefits such as retirement plans (e.g., 401(k), SEP IRA), health insurance plans, and flexible spending accounts (FSAs). These benefits can be tax-deductible for the business and provide tax advantages for employees.

**Research and Development (R&D) Tax Credits:**

If your business engages in qualifying research and development activities, explore the potential eligibility for R&D tax credits. These credits can help offset the costs associated with innovation and product development.

**Depreciation and Asset Write-Offs:**

Take advantage of accelerated depreciation methods and asset write-offs to minimize taxable income. Section 179 deductions and bonus depreciation provisions may allow for upfront expensing of certain business assets.

**Tax Credits and Incentives:**

Identify and leverage applicable tax credits and incentives specific to your industry or location. Examples include energy-efficient tax credits, investment tax credits, or job creation incentives.

**State and Local Taxes:**

Understand the state and local tax laws and consider locating your business in jurisdictions with favourable tax climates. Some states offer tax incentives for businesses, such as tax credits for job creation or exemptions for certain industries.

**International Tax Optimization:**

For businesses engaged in international operations or individuals with international income or investments, international tax optimization strategies can be crucial. Consider the following approaches:

### Tax Treaties:

Understand the tax treaties between countries to avoid double taxation and take advantage of any benefits or exemptions provided.

### Transfer Pricing:

Comply with transfer pricing rules to ensure that transactions between related entities in different jurisdictions are priced appropriately. This helps prevent tax authorities from challenging the pricing and potentially imposing penalties or adjustments.

### Offshore Structures:

If your business operates internationally, explore the use of offshore structures to optimize your tax position. Offshore entities can provide tax advantages such as reduced tax rates, tax deferral, or asset protection.

### Foreign Tax Credits:

If you have foreign income subject to taxation, consider claiming foreign tax credits to offset the tax paid in foreign jurisdictions against your domestic tax liability.

### Controlled Foreign Corporation (CFC) Rules:

Be aware of CFC rules that apply to certain foreign corporations owned by U.S. shareholders. Compliance with these rules is essential to ensure that income earned through these entities is appropriately reported and taxed.

**Tax Planning for Investments:**

Investment tax planning strategies can help individuals minimize taxes on investment income and capital gains. Consider the following approaches:

**Tax-Efficient Asset Allocation:**

Allocate your investments across different accounts based on their tax efficiency. For example, consider holding tax-efficient investments in taxable accounts and tax-inefficient investments in tax-advantaged accounts.

**Tax-Loss Harvesting:**

Offset capital gains with capital losses by strategically selling investments that have declined in value. This can help reduce your taxable capital gains.

**Asset Location:**

Place investments in the appropriate account type to maximize tax efficiency. For example, hold income-generating investments, such as bonds or REITs, in tax-advantaged accounts to defer taxes on the income.

### Qualified Dividends and Long-Term Capital Gains:

Understand the tax advantages of qualified dividends and long-term capital gains, which are typically taxed at lower rates than ordinary income. Consider holding investments that generate these types of income to benefit from lower tax rates.

### Tax-Advantaged Investment Accounts:

Maximize contributions to tax-advantaged accounts such as IRAs, 401(k)s, or Health Savings Accounts (HSAs). These accounts offer tax benefits such as tax-deductible contributions, tax-deferred growth, or tax-free withdrawals for qualified expenses.

### Tax-Loss Carry forwards:

Utilize tax-loss carry forwards from previous years to offset future capital gains. If you have unused capital losses, they can be carried forward to offset future gains and potentially reduce your tax liability.

### Conclusion:

Tax optimization strategies play a crucial role in preserving and maximizing your wealth. By understanding the tax landscape, implementing effective income tax planning strategies, optimizing business tax structures, exploring international tax considerations, and employing investment tax planning techniques, you can minimize your tax liability and optimize your financial position. However, tax optimization should always be approached within the boundaries of the law and with the guidance of qualified tax professionals to ensure compliance and effectiveness. Regular reviews and adaptations to your tax optimization strategies are essential to reflect changes in tax laws, your financial situation, and evolving tax planning opportunities. Consult with a tax advisor or financial planner to tailor these strategies to your specific circumstances and objectives, ensuring that you optimize your taxes while remaining compliant with applicable tax laws and regulations.

## 9.3    Wealth Management and Financial Advisors

Wealth management is a comprehensive approach to financial planning that focuses on preserving and growing an individual's or family's wealth over the long term. It involves strategic management of assets, investments, taxes, estate planning, and risk management. Wealth management aims to help individuals achieve their financial goals and ensure the long-term sustainability and prosperity of their wealth. Financial advisors play a crucial role in providing expert guidance and customized strategies to navigate the complexities of wealth management. In this guide, we will explore the concept of wealth management, the role of financial advisors, and the key components of a robust wealth management plan.

**Understanding Wealth Management:**

Wealth management goes beyond simple investment management. It takes a holistic view of an individual's financial situation, considering various aspects of their financial life. Key elements of wealth management include:

**Financial Goal Setting:**

Identifying and prioritizing short-term and long-term financial goals, such as retirement planning, education funding, legacy planning, or lifestyle aspirations.

**Risk Assessment and Management:**

Evaluating the individual's risk tolerance, assessing potential risks to their wealth, and developing strategies to mitigate those risks through insurance, asset diversification, and other risk management techniques.

**Investment Management:**

Developing a customized investment strategy that aligns with the individual's goals, risk tolerance, and time horizon. This includes asset allocation, portfolio diversification, investment selection, and regular monitoring and rebalancing.

**Tax Planning:**

Implementing strategies to minimize tax liability through effective tax planning, taking advantage of available tax incentives, and optimizing investment structures to minimize taxable income and capital gains.

**Estate Planning:**

Ensuring the orderly distribution of assets according to the individual's wishes and minimizing estate taxes through strategies such as trusts, wills, beneficiary designations, and charitable giving.

**Cash Flow Management:**

Developing a comprehensive budgeting and cash flow plan to effectively manage income, expenses, and savings, ensuring that financial resources are allocated efficiently and in line with goals.

**Risk Management and Insurance:**

Assessing insurance needs, including life insurance, health insurance, property and casualty insurance, and liability coverage, to protect against unforeseen events and potential financial losses.

**The Role of Financial Advisors:**

Financial advisors are professionals who provide expert guidance and advice on various aspects of wealth management. They help individuals navigate complex financial decisions, develop personalized strategies, and monitor progress towards financial goals. The key roles and responsibilities of financial advisors include:

**Comprehensive Financial Assessment:**

Conducting an in-depth analysis of the individual's financial situation, goals, risk tolerance, and time horizon to gain a holistic understanding of their unique circumstances.

**Customized Wealth Management Plan:**

Developing a tailored wealth management plan that encompasses investment strategies, tax planning, estate planning, risk management, and other relevant components based on the individual's objectives.

**Investment Advisory Services:**

Providing investment advice and portfolio management services to help individuals make informed investment decisions, diversify their portfolios, and achieve their financial objectives.

**Financial Goal Setting:**

Assisting individuals in setting realistic and achievable financial goals, both short-term and long-term, and developing strategies to track progress and make adjustments as needed.

**Regular Monitoring and Review:**

Continuously monitoring the individual's financial situation, investment performance, and progress towards goals. Conducting regular reviews and making adjustments to the wealth management plan as circumstances change.

**Education and Guidance:**

Educating individuals about financial concepts, investment options, and strategies, empowering them to make informed decisions and build financial literacy.

**Coordination with Other Professionals:**

Collaborating with other professionals, such as tax advisors, estate planners, and attorneys, to ensure a cohesive and integrated approach to wealth management.

**Behavioural Coaching:**

Guiding individuals through market fluctuations, helping them avoid emotional decision-making, and providing objective advice to stay focused on long-term goals.

**Components of a Robust Wealth Management Plan:**

A robust wealth management plan encompasses several key components that work together to achieve financial goals and preserve and grow wealth. Consider the following components:

**Financial Goal Setting:**

Clearly defining short-term and long-term financial goals and aligning investment strategies and planning efforts accordingly.

**Investment Strategy and Asset Allocation:**

Developing a customized investment strategy that reflects the individual's risk tolerance, time horizon, and financial goals. Implementing a diversified asset allocation strategy that balances risk and return.

**Tax Planning and Optimization:**

Utilizing tax-efficient investment strategies, taking advantage of available tax deductions and credits, and optimizing investment structures to minimize tax liabilities.

**Estate Planning:**

Creating an estate plan that includes wills, trusts, beneficiary designations, and powers of attorney to ensure the orderly transfer of assets, minimize estate taxes, and protect family wealth.

**Risk Management and Insurance:**

Assessing risk exposure and implementing appropriate insurance coverage to protect against potential risks and financial losses.

**Retirement Planning:**

Developing a comprehensive retirement plan that includes savings strategies, investment allocation, and income projections to ensure a comfortable retirement.

**Education Funding:**

Planning for education expenses, such as college tuition, by utilizing tax-advantaged accounts, scholarship opportunities, and savings strategies.

**Charitable Giving:**

Incorporating philanthropic goals into the wealth management plan by developing strategies for charitable giving and optimizing the impact of charitable donations.

**Regular Monitoring and Adjustments:**

Continuously monitoring investment performance, reviewing progress towards financial goals, and making adjustments as needed to ensure alignment with changing circumstances.

**Conclusion:**

Wealth management is a comprehensive approach to financial planning that encompasses various aspects of an individual's financial life. It involves strategic management of assets, investments, taxes, estate planning, risk management, and more. Financial advisors play a crucial role in guiding individuals through the complexities of wealth management, providing expertise, personalized advice, and ongoing support. By developing a robust wealth management plan that aligns with their goals, risk tolerance, and financial circumstances, individuals can optimize their financial position, achieve their objectives, and secure long-term financial well-being. Regular monitoring, adjustments, and collaboration with professionals ensure that the plan remains relevant and effective as circumstances change.

## 9.4 Philanthropy and Giving Back

Philanthropy and giving back play a vital role in society by promoting social welfare, addressing pressing issues, and creating positive change. Philanthropy involves the act of giving one's time, resources, or expertise to support charitable causes and make a meaningful impact on the lives of others. Whether through financial contributions, volunteer work, or advocacy efforts, philanthropy provides individuals and organizations with an opportunity to give back and contribute to the betterment of society. In this guide, we will explore the concept of philanthropy, its benefits, various forms of giving back, and how to engage in effective philanthropic efforts.

**Understanding Philanthropy:**

Philanthropy is rooted in the desire to improve the well-being of others and make a positive difference in society. It involves voluntarily giving one's resources, such as money, time, skills, or influence, to support causes that align with one's values and passions. Philanthropy can take various forms, including:

**Financial Contributions:**

Donating money or assets to charitable organizations, nonprofits, foundations, or community initiatives. This can involve one-time donations, recurring contributions, or establishing endowed funds.

**Volunteerism:**

Offering one's time, skills, or expertise to support charitable organizations and actively participate in community service. This can include volunteering at local nonprofits, participating in service projects, or serving on boards of charitable organizations.

**Advocacy and Activism:**

Engaging in advocacy efforts to raise awareness, influence public opinion, and advocate for policy changes related to social, environmental, or humanitarian causes.

**Impact Investing:**

Deploying investment capital with the intention of generating both financial returns and positive social or environmental impact. This approach aligns investment decisions with philanthropic goals.

**Corporate Social Responsibility:**

Businesses engaging in philanthropic activities as part of their social responsibility efforts. This can involve corporate donations, employee volunteer programs, sustainable business practices, or partnerships with nonprofits.

### Benefits of Philanthropy:

Philanthropy brings numerous benefits to both individuals and society as a whole. Consider the following advantages:

### Fulfillment and Purpose:

Engaging in philanthropy provides a sense of purpose and fulfillment by making a positive impact and contributing to the well-being of others.

### Social Impact:

Philanthropic efforts can address pressing social issues, improve living conditions, support education, promote health and well-being, and advance social justice causes.

### Community Building:

Philanthropy strengthens communities by fostering connections, encouraging collaboration, and bringing people together to work towards common goals.

### Personal Growth:

Engaging in philanthropy offers opportunities for personal growth, development, and learning. It broadens perspectives, cultivates empathy, and enhances leadership and problem-solving skills.

### Networking and Relationships:

Philanthropy provides opportunities to connect with like-minded individuals, form meaningful relationships, and collaborate with others who share similar passions and values.

### Legacy and Family Values:

Philanthropy allows individuals to establish a legacy and pass on their values to future generations. It can create a lasting impact that extends beyond one's lifetime.

### Forms of Giving Back:

Philanthropy and giving back can take various forms, depending on personal preferences, resources, and interests. Consider the following ways to engage in giving back:

### Financial Donations:

Make financial contributions to charitable organizations, nonprofits, or community initiatives. This can involve supporting causes such as education, healthcare, poverty alleviation, environmental conservation, arts and culture, or disaster relief.

### Volunteer Work:

Dedicate time and skills to support charitable organizations. This can involve serving meals at a food bank, tutoring students, assisting in community clean-up projects, or offering professional expertise to nonprofits.

### Mentoring and Education:

Provide guidance, mentorship, or educational support to individuals or organizations. This can include mentoring youth, teaching skills or workshops, or supporting scholarships and educational programs.

### Pro Bono Services:

Offer professional services or expertise on a pro bono basis to nonprofits or individuals who may not have the resources to access such services otherwise. This can include legal advice, financial planning, marketing assistance, or strategic consulting.

### Cause-Related Fundraising:

Organize or participate in fundraising events or campaigns to raise funds and awareness for specific causes or charities. This can include charity runs, auctions, benefit concerts, or crowdfunding campaigns.

### Advocacy and Awareness:

Use your voice and platform to advocate for social causes, raise awareness about important issues, and support policy changes that promote positive change.

### Effective Philanthropic Efforts:

To ensure effective and impactful philanthropy, consider the following strategies:

### Define Your Philanthropic Goals:

Clarify your values, passions, and areas of interest. Determine the causes or issues you are most passionate about and where you believe your contributions can make the most significant impact.

### Research and Due Diligence:

Conduct thorough research on charitable organizations or initiatives you wish to support. Assess their track record, transparency, governance, and the impact of their work. Consider partnering with reputable organizations that align with your values.

### Engage in Strategic Giving:

Develop a philanthropic plan that outlines your giving strategy, including the amount, frequency, and areas of focus. Consider focusing your giving on a few key causes to maximize impact and build deeper relationships with the organizations you support.

### Collaborate and Leverage Resources:

Collaborate with other philanthropists, organizations, or community stakeholders to leverage resources and collectively address social challenges. Engage in partnerships and collaborations to amplify impact.

**Measurement and Evaluation:**

Regularly evaluate the impact of your philanthropic efforts. Set measurable goals and metrics to assess the effectiveness of your contributions. Use this information to refine your strategies and make informed decisions about future giving.

**Long-Term and Sustainable Approaches:**

Consider supporting initiatives that aim to create long-term, sustainable change. This can involve investing in education, capacity-building, or systemic change efforts that address the root causes of social issues.

**Continual Learning and Adaptation:**

Stay informed about emerging social issues, innovative approaches, and best practices in philanthropy. Continually educate yourself about the causes you support and adapt your giving strategies based on new insights and evolving needs.

**Conclusion:**

Philanthropy and giving back are powerful ways to create positive change and make a lasting impact on society. Whether through financial contributions, volunteer work, advocacy efforts, or strategic partnerships, individuals and organizations have the ability to address social challenges, support community development, and improve the lives of others. Engaging in philanthropy not only benefits those in need but also provides personal fulfillment, strengthens communities, and promotes a sense of social responsibility. By adopting effective philanthropic strategies, conducting due diligence, collaborating with others, and evaluating impact, individuals can make a meaningful difference and contribute to a more just and compassionate world.

# 10.    Celebrating Financial Independence

Financial independence is a significant milestone in one's life, representing the ability to sustainably support oneself and achieve financial goals without being dependent on others. It provides individuals with the freedom to make choices that align with their values, pursue their passions, and live life on their own terms. Celebrating financial independence is an opportunity to reflect on one's achievements, acknowledge the hard work and discipline that led to this point, and set new goals for the future. In this guide, we will explore the importance of celebrating financial independence, various ways to commemorate this milestone, and how to maintain financial independence over the long term.

## 10.1    Achieving the $1,000,000 Milestone

Reaching the $1,000,000 milestone is a significant accomplishment on the journey to financial independence and wealth accumulation. It represents a substantial amount of savings and investment growth that can provide individuals with greater financial security, freedom, and opportunities. Achieving this milestone requires a combination of disciplined saving, smart investment strategies, and a long-term perspective. In this guide, we will explore key principles and strategies to help you reach the $1,000,000 milestone and set a solid foundation for financial success.

**Set Clear Financial Goals:**

To achieve the $1,000,000 milestone, it is essential to set clear financial goals. Consider the following steps:

**Define Your Objective:**

Clarify why you want to reach the $1,000,000 milestone. Is it for financial security, early retirement, starting a business, or funding a particular goal or dream? Understanding your motivations will help you stay focused and committed throughout the journey.

**Quantify Your Target:**

Determine the exact amount you need to reach $1,000,000. Consider any additional factors, such as inflation or specific timeframes, to ensure your goal is realistic and achievable.

**Break It Down:**

Divide your target into smaller, manageable milestones. Setting incremental goals can provide a sense of progress and make the overall journey less overwhelming.

**Create a Timeline:**

Establish a timeline for reaching your $1,000,000 goal. This will help you stay on track and provide a sense of urgency to take consistent action towards your objective.

**Implement Effective Saving Strategies:**

Saving is a crucial component of reaching the $1,000,000 milestone. Consider the following strategies:

**Budgeting:**

Create a detailed budget to track your income and expenses. Identify areas where you can reduce unnecessary spending and allocate those savings towards your goal.

**Pay Yourself First:**

Prioritize saving by automating regular contributions to your savings and investment accounts. Treat saving as an essential expense and allocate a percentage of your income before allocating funds to other discretionary expenses.

**Reduce Debt:**

Minimize high-interest debt, such as credit card debt or personal loans. Allocating resources towards debt repayment will free up additional funds for saving and investing.

**Increase Income:**

Explore opportunities to increase your income, such as negotiating a raise, starting a side business, or taking on additional freelance work. The additional income can accelerate your progress towards the $1,000,000 milestone.

**Embrace Frugality:**

Adopt a frugal mindset and find ways to save money in daily life. Cut unnecessary expenses, shop for deals, and seek out cost-saving measures without sacrificing your quality of life.

**Invest Strategically:**

Investing wisely is crucial for growing your wealth and reaching the $1,000,000 milestone. Consider the following investment strategies:

**Diversification:**

Spread your investments across different asset classes, such as stocks, bonds, real estate, and mutual funds, to reduce risk and increase potential returns.

**Long-Term Perspective:**

Embrace a long-term investment approach and resist the temptation to make impulsive decisions based on short-term market fluctuations. Maintain a disciplined investment strategy aligned with your risk tolerance and goals.

**Maximize Tax-Advantaged Accounts:**

Contribute to tax-advantaged accounts such as 401(k)s, IRAs, or HSAs. These accounts offer tax benefits, such as tax-deferred growth or tax-free withdrawals, allowing your investments to compound more efficiently.

**Regular Contributions:**

Consistently contribute to your investment accounts. Regular contributions, even small ones, can accumulate over time and benefit from compounding returns.

**Seek Professional Advice:**

Consider working with a financial advisor or investment professional to guide you through the investment process, assess your risk tolerance, and develop a tailored investment strategy that aligns with your goals.

**Minimize Taxes:**

Minimizing taxes is a key aspect of wealth accumulation. Consider the following tax optimization strategies:

**Utilize Tax Deductions:**

Take advantage of tax deductions, such as those related to mortgage interest, education expenses, or charitable contributions. Be aware of available tax incentives and deductions that can help reduce your taxable income.

**Tax-Efficient Investments:**

Opt for tax-efficient investment vehicles, such as index funds or exchange-traded funds (ETFs), which generate minimal taxable distributions. This can help minimize the tax impact on your investment returns.

**Capital Gains Strategies:**

Consider tax-efficient strategies for realizing capital gains, such as tax-loss harvesting, which involves selling investments that have declined in value to offset capital gains.

**Maximize Retirement Contributions:**

Contribute the maximum allowable amounts to tax-advantaged retirement accounts. Not only will this help secure your financial future, but it will also provide immediate tax benefits.

**Consider Tax-Deferred Investments:**

Explore tax-deferred investment options, such as annuities or cash-value life insurance policies, to defer taxes on investment gains.

### Stay Committed and Adapt:

Reaching the $1,000,000 milestone requires discipline, patience, and adaptability. Consider the following principles:

### Stay Committed to Your Goals:

Maintain a strong commitment to your financial objectives. Stay motivated by regularly reviewing your progress, celebrating milestones along the way, and reminding yourself of the benefits and rewards that come with achieving financial independence.

### Stay Educated and Informed:

Continually educate yourself about personal finance and investment strategies. Stay up-to-date with market trends, tax regulations, and financial news to make informed decisions about your investments.

### Adjust Your Plan as Needed:

Be flexible and willing to adapt your strategies as circumstances change. Life events, market conditions, or personal goals may require adjustments to your savings and investment plan. Regularly review and reassess your approach to ensure it remains aligned with your objectives.

**Seek Professional Advice:**

Consider working with a financial advisor or wealth management professional to help you navigate complex financial decisions, provide expert guidance, and ensure that your strategies remain aligned with your goals.

**Conclusion:**

Reaching the $1,000,000 milestone is an achievement that signifies financial security, freedom, and the potential for greater opportunities. By setting clear goals, implementing effective saving and investing strategies, minimizing taxes, and maintaining a long-term perspective, you can make significant progress towards this milestone. Remember that reaching $1,000,000 is not an overnight success but rather a journey that requires commitment, discipline, and adaptability. Stay focused, celebrate milestones along the way, and continue to educate yourself about personal finance and investment strategies. With perseverance and strategic planning, you can achieve the $1,000,000 milestone and set a solid foundation for long-term financial success and independence.

## 10.2    Enjoying the Fruits of Financial Freedom

Financial freedom is a goal many strive to achieve, representing a state of financial security and independence that allows individuals to enjoy the fruits of their labor. It provides the freedom to make choices aligned with personal values, pursue passions, and create a fulfilling and abundant life. Once financial freedom is attained, it is essential to embrace and enjoy the newfound benefits responsibly. In this guide, we will explore various ways to enjoy the fruits of financial freedom while maintaining financial well-being and long-term sustainability.

**Embrace a Balanced Lifestyle:**

One of the key aspects of enjoying financial freedom is finding balance in your lifestyle. Consider the following approaches:

**Prioritize Experiences over Material Possessions:**

Focus on creating meaningful experiences and memories rather than solely accumulating material possessions. Travel, explore new hobbies, spend time with loved ones, and engage in activities that bring you joy and fulfillment.

**Practice Mindful Spending:**

Be intentional with your spending by aligning your expenses with your values and goals. Consider the value and impact of each purchase, ensuring that it enhances your well-being and aligns with your long-term objectives.

**Avoid Lifestyle Inflation:**

Resist the urge to dramatically increase your expenses and lifestyle upon achieving financial freedom. Instead, maintain a level of spending that aligns with your values and long-term financial sustainability.

**Give Back and Support Causes:**

Engage in philanthropy and charitable giving to support causes that resonate with you. Use your financial freedom to make a positive impact in the world and contribute to the well-being of others.

**Pursue Personal Growth and Learning:**

Financial freedom provides the opportunity to invest in personal growth and lifelong learning. Consider the following approaches:

**Invest in Education and Skills:**

Use your resources to further your education, develop new skills, or pursue certifications that can enhance your personal and professional growth. Continually invest in self-improvement to expand your horizons and open up new opportunities.

### Explore Passions and Hobbies:

Dedicate time and resources to explore and cultivate your passions and hobbies. Whether it's art, music, sports, or any other pursuit, allow yourself the freedom to immerse yourself in activities that bring you joy and fulfillment.

### Engage in Personal Development:

Attend seminars, workshops, or retreats focused on personal development and self-discovery. This can help you deepen your self-awareness, enhance your mindset, and unlock your full potential.

### Travel and Cultural Experiences:

Take advantage of your financial freedom to explore different cultures, travel to new destinations, and broaden your horizons. Travel can provide valuable experiences, foster personal growth, and create lifelong memories.

### Create Meaningful Relationships:

Financial freedom can enable you to cultivate and nurture meaningful relationships. Consider the following approaches:

### Spend Quality Time with Loved Ones:

Prioritize spending quality time with family and friends. Foster deep connections and create lasting memories through shared experiences, travel, or simply spending time together.

**Strengthen Community Engagement:**

Contribute to your community and engage in activities that benefit others. Volunteer, participate in community projects, or join organizations that align with your values and allow you to connect with like-minded individuals.

**Support Loved Ones:**

Use your financial resources to support and uplift your loved ones. Whether it's assisting family members in need, funding educational opportunities for children, or helping friends achieve their goals, supporting those close to you can deepen relationships and bring joy.

**Maintain Financial Wellness:**

While enjoying the fruits of financial freedom, it is crucial to maintain financial wellness and long-term sustainability. Consider the following strategies:

**Stick to a Financial Plan:**

Continue to follow a financial plan and budget that aligns with your goals. Regularly review and assess your financial situation to ensure that you stay on track and maintain a healthy financial position.

### Preserve an Emergency Fund:

Maintain an emergency fund to cover unforeseen expenses or unexpected events. This provides a safety net and protects your financial well-being in case of emergencies.

### Focus on Long-Term Investments:

Allocate resources towards long-term investments that can continue to grow and provide income in the future. Diversify your investment portfolio and seek professional advice to ensure your investments remain aligned with your long-term goals.

### Practice Risk Management:

Protect your assets and income through adequate insurance coverage. Evaluate your insurance needs and ensure that you have appropriate coverage for health, property, liability, and other potential risks.

### Estate Planning:

Establish an estate plan to ensure the orderly transfer of your assets and protect your wealth for future generations. Consult with legal and financial professionals to create a comprehensive plan that aligns with your wishes.

### Give Back and Make a Difference:

Financial freedom provides a unique opportunity to give back to society and make a positive impact. Consider the following approaches:

### Philanthropy and Charitable Giving:

Use your financial resources to support causes that are meaningful to you. Engage in philanthropic efforts, donate to charitable organizations, or establish your own charitable foundation to create lasting change.

### Mentorship and Volunteerism:

Share your knowledge, skills, and experiences by mentoring others or engaging in volunteer work. Contribute to the development and growth of individuals and communities through your time and expertise.

### Advocacy and Social Responsibility:

Use your voice and influence to advocate for social and environmental issues that matter to you. Support initiatives that promote sustainability, equality, and positive change in the world.

### Conclusion:

Achieving financial freedom is a significant accomplishment, and it opens up a world of opportunities to enjoy life, pursue passions, and make a difference. By embracing a balanced lifestyle, investing in personal growth, nurturing relationships, maintaining financial wellness, and giving back to society, you can fully enjoy the fruits of financial freedom while ensuring long-term sustainability. Remember that financial freedom is not just about accumulating wealth but also about finding purpose, fulfillment, and happiness in the choices you make and the impact you create.

## 10.3    Legacy Building and Long-Term Planning

Legacy building and long-term planning are essential components of financial management that go beyond personal wealth accumulation. They involve considering the impact you can have on future generations, the causes you care about, and the preservation of your values and assets. Legacy building is about leaving a lasting and meaningful impact on the world, while long-term planning ensures the sustainability and smooth transition of your wealth and values. In this guide, we will explore the importance of legacy building and long-term planning, the key elements involved, and strategies to effectively implement them.

**Understanding Legacy Building:**

Legacy building involves creating a lasting impact that extends beyond an individual's lifetime. It is about leaving a positive imprint on the world and future generations by sharing your values, knowledge, resources, and experiences. Consider the following aspects:

**Values and Principles:**

Identify and define the core values and principles that guide your life. These principles serve as a foundation for your legacy and provide a framework for decision-making and the impact you want to have.

### Impact Areas:

Reflect on the areas of life or specific causes that you are passionate about and where you want to make a difference. This can be related to education, healthcare, social justice, environmental conservation, arts and culture, or any other area that aligns with your values.

### Philanthropy and Charitable Giving:

Philanthropy is a powerful way to build a legacy. Consider supporting charitable organizations or establishing your own foundation to continue your philanthropic efforts even after you are gone. Leave a lasting impact by supporting causes that reflect your values and have long-term benefits.

### Mentorship and Knowledge Sharing:

Pass on your knowledge, skills, and experiences to future generations. Mentoring others, sharing your expertise, and promoting lifelong learning can have a profound impact on individuals and society as a whole.

### Importance of Long-Term Planning:

Long-term planning ensures the efficient management and preservation of your wealth and values. It involves considering the future and implementing strategies to safeguard your assets, provide for your loved ones, and address potential challenges. Consider the following elements:

**Estate Planning:**

Develop an estate plan that outlines how your assets will be distributed after your passing. This includes creating a will, establishing trusts, designating beneficiaries, and appointing guardians for dependents. Estate planning ensures that your assets are transferred according to your wishes and minimizes potential conflicts.

**Succession Planning:**

If you own a business or have significant assets, consider succession planning to ensure a smooth transition of ownership and management. This involves identifying and preparing successors, outlining roles and responsibilities, and providing for the continuation of the business or asset management.

**Risk Management:**

Implement strategies to mitigate risks and protect your assets. This includes obtaining appropriate insurance coverage, considering asset protection structures, and developing contingency plans to address potential challenges.

**Tax Planning:**

Engage in tax planning to minimize tax liabilities and maximize the value of your estate. This can involve utilizing tax-efficient investment vehicles, taking advantage of available tax deductions, and considering charitable giving strategies to reduce potential estate taxes.

**Health Care Planning:**

Consider long-term care and healthcare planning to ensure that your medical needs are met as you age. This includes having health insurance coverage, creating advanced healthcare directives, and establishing powers of attorney for healthcare decisions.

**Strategies for Legacy Building and Long-Term Planning:**

Implementing effective strategies is key to successful legacy building and long-term planning. Consider the following approaches:

**Engage Professional Advisors:**

Seek guidance from professionals such as estate planners, financial advisors, tax experts, and lawyers who specialize in legacy planning. They can provide expertise and help you navigate complex legal and financial matters.

**Develop a Comprehensive Plan:**

Create a comprehensive plan that encompasses all aspects of your legacy and long-term goals. This includes financial considerations, charitable giving, family dynamics, business succession, and asset protection. Regularly review and update your plan as circumstances change.

**Communicate and Involve Family Members:**

Involve your loved ones in the planning process and openly communicate your intentions and values. This ensures that everyone is aware of your wishes, reduces the potential for conflicts, and allows for a smoother transition of wealth and responsibilities.

**Continual Education and Learning:**

Stay informed about changes in laws, financial regulations, and investment strategies. Continually educate yourself on best practices in estate planning, philanthropy, and wealth management to ensure your strategies remain effective and up to date.

**Consider Philanthropic Options:**

Explore different philanthropic options to leave a lasting impact. This can include establishing a family foundation, donor-advised funds, or contributing to existing charitable organizations. Seek opportunities to engage future generations in philanthropy and promote family values.

**Review and Update Regularly:**

Regularly review and update your plans to ensure they remain aligned with your current circumstances, goals, and values. Life events, changes in financial situations, or shifts in priorities may require adjustments to your long-term planning and legacy building strategies.

**Conclusion:**

Legacy building and long-term planning are critical components of a comprehensive financial management strategy. They involve considering the impact you want to have on future generations, the causes you care about, and the smooth transition of your wealth and values. By engaging in philanthropy, implementing effective long-term planning strategies, involving professional advisors, and communicating with loved ones, you can create a lasting legacy that reflects your values and ensures the sustainability of your wealth for generations to come. Remember that legacy building is not just about financial considerations but also about the impact you have on individuals, communities, and the world.

## 10.4    Inspiring Others and Sharing Knowledge

Inspiring others and sharing knowledge is a powerful way to make a positive impact on individuals, communities, and society as a whole. By imparting wisdom, insights, and experiences, you have the ability to motivate, educate, and empower others to reach their full potential. Inspiring and sharing knowledge not only benefits those who receive it but also creates a ripple effect, as inspired individuals go on to inspire others. In this guide, we will explore the importance of inspiring others and sharing knowledge, the benefits it brings, and strategies to effectively inspire and educate.

**The Power of Inspiration:**

Inspiration has the ability to ignite passion, drive, and motivation within individuals. It sparks a sense of possibility and encourages people to pursue their dreams and aspirations. Consider the following aspects:

**Motivation:**

Inspiration provides the motivation and drive needed to overcome challenges, push through obstacles, and persist in the pursuit of goals. It fuels a sense of determination and resilience.

**Empowerment:**

When individuals are inspired, they feel empowered to take action and make positive changes in their lives.

Inspiration instils belief in one's abilities and encourages individuals to step out of their comfort zones.

**Positive Mindset:**

Inspiration cultivates a positive mindset, fostering optimism, creativity, and a solution-oriented approach. It helps individuals see opportunities where others see limitations.

**Personal Growth:**

Inspired individuals are more likely to engage in personal growth and self-improvement. They seek out new knowledge, skills, and experiences that align with their inspired vision.

**Sharing Knowledge:**

Sharing knowledge involves imparting information, insights, and expertise to others. It allows individuals to learn from one another, benefit from collective wisdom, and accelerate their personal growth. Consider the following benefits:

**Empowering Others:**

Sharing knowledge empowers individuals by providing them with the tools, information, and perspectives they need to make informed decisions and take meaningful action.

**Fostering Growth and Development:**

Knowledge sharing fosters personal growth and development by expanding individuals' understanding, skills, and capabilities. It helps them acquire new knowledge and perspectives that can contribute to their success.

**Building Stronger Communities:**

When knowledge is shared within communities, it strengthens social bonds, fosters collaboration, and promotes the collective well-being. It enables individuals to support and learn from one another, leading to the growth and development of the community as a whole.

**Creating Innovation and Progress:**

Knowledge sharing is the foundation of innovation and progress. By sharing insights, ideas, and experiences, individuals can build upon existing knowledge and collectively solve complex problems.

**Strategies for Inspiring Others:**

Inspiring others is a powerful way to ignite motivation and drive within individuals. Consider the following strategies to effectively inspire others:

**Lead by Example:**

Be a role model by embodying the qualities, values, and behaviours you want to inspire in others.

Demonstrate integrity, resilience, empathy, and a growth mindset in your own actions.

**Share Personal Stories:**

Stories have the power to connect with people on an emotional level. Share your personal stories of triumph, perseverance, and overcoming challenges to inspire and motivate others.

**Set Realistic Goals:**

Help individuals set realistic and achievable goals that align with their passions and values. Encourage them to step outside their comfort zones and take incremental steps towards their objectives.

**Provide Support and Encouragement:**

Offer support, encouragement, and constructive feedback to individuals as they pursue their goals. Be a source of motivation and guidance throughout their journey.

**Celebrate Success:**

Acknowledge and celebrate the successes, milestones, and achievements of others. Recognize their efforts and inspire them to keep pushing forward.

**Strategies for Sharing Knowledge:**

Sharing knowledge effectively involves conveying information in a way that is accessible, engaging, and impactful. Consider the following strategies to share knowledge effectively:

**Tailor Communication to the Audience:**

Adapt your message and delivery to suit the needs, interests, and learning styles of your audience. Use relatable examples, stories, and visuals to enhance understanding and engagement.

**Be Clear and Concise:**

Present information in a clear and concise manner, avoiding unnecessary jargon or complexity. Break down complex concepts into digestible pieces and use simple language to ensure comprehension.

**Use Multiple Channels:**

Utilize various communication channels to reach a broader audience. This can include written materials, presentations, workshops, webinars, podcasts, or social media platforms.

**Encourage Discussion and Collaboration:**

Foster a collaborative learning environment by encouraging discussion, questions, and active participation. Create opportunities for individuals to share their perspectives, insights, and experiences.

**Provide Practical Applications:**

Connect theoretical knowledge with practical applications to enhance relevance and utility. Help individuals understand how they can apply the knowledge in their personal and professional lives.

**Continual Learning and Improvement:**

Commit to continual learning and improvement in your own knowledge and skills. Stay up-to-date with the latest research, trends, and developments in your field to provide the most accurate and relevant information.

**Conclusion:**

Inspiring others and sharing knowledge are powerful ways to make a positive impact on individuals, communities, and society. By inspiring and empowering others, you contribute to their personal growth, motivation, and success. Sharing knowledge enhances collective wisdom, fosters innovation, and accelerates progress. Through leading by example, sharing personal stories, setting realistic goals, and providing support, you can effectively inspire others. Similarly, tailoring communication, being clear and concise, encouraging discussion, and providing practical applications enable you to share knowledge effectively. Remember that inspiration and knowledge sharing are ongoing processes, requiring commitment, empathy, and a genuine desire to empower and uplift others.

www.ingramcontent.com/pod-product-compliance
Lightning Source LLC
Chambersburg PA
CBHW072137290526
45794CB00004B/1348